The Grand Tour of Park Ex

& Assorted Half-Told Yarns

MIROLAND IMPRINT 49

Canada

Canada Council for the Arts | Conseil des arts du Canada

Guernica Editions Inc. acknowledges the support
of the Canada Council for the Arts and the Ontario Arts Council.
The Ontario Arts Council is an agency of the Government of Ontario.
We acknowledge the financial support of the Government of Canada.

ANDREAS KESSARIS

The Grand Tour of Park Ex

& Assorted Half-Told Yarns

MiroLand
publishers

TORONTO • CHICAGO • BUFFALO • LANCASTER (U.K.)
2025

Guernica Founder: Antonio D'Alfonso

Michael Mirolla, general editor
Gary Clairman, editor
Cover design and interior design: Rafael Chimicatti
Front Cover Image: Peter Kessaris

Guernica Editions Inc.
1241 Marble Rock Rd., Gananoque, ON K7G 2V4
2250 Military Road, Tonawanda, N.Y. 14150-6000 U.S.A.
www.guernicaeditions.com

Distributors:
Independent Publishers Group (IPG)
600 North Pulaski Road, Chicago IL 60624
University of Toronto Press Distribution (UTP)
5201 Dufferin Street, Toronto (ON), Canada M3H 5T8

First edition.
Printed in Canada.

Legal Deposit—Third Quarter
Library of Congress Catalog Card Number: 2024948808
Library and Archives Canada Cataloguing in Publication
Title: The grand tour of Park Ex & assorted half-told yarns / Andreas Kessaris.
Other titles: Grand tour of Park Ex and assorted half-told yarns
Names: Kessaris, Andreas, author.
Description: "MiroLand imprint, 49"--Page preceding title page.
Identifiers: Canadiana (print) 20240501128 | Canadiana (ebook) 20240507746 |
ISBN 9781771839730 (softcover) | ISBN 9781771839747 (EPUB)
Subjects: LCGFT: Short stories.
Classification: LCC PS8621.E86 G73 2025 | DDC C813/.6—dc23

For Kelly

To Richard King

CONTENTS

Author's Note

Although based on actual incidents, the following stories may contain embellishments, hyperbole is at times generously applied, some situations are amalgams or fictionalizations, a number of names have been changed, and certain characters are composites. Instances depicted are as I remember or perceive them, not as they might have factually transpired. Opinions expressed are mine alone and not necessarily those of the publisher, editor, distributor, or anyone else associated with me or this book in any way, shape or form. This book was not written with the intention of hurting, insulting, shaming, or otherwise burning any specific person or group of people. Read at your own risk. People who are easily offended should stop right here.

For those of you who wish to continue on this journey with me, I offer my humble gratitude for your understanding. I sincerely hope you enjoy the ride.

PARTICIPANT

When my nephew turned four my mother decided it was time she learned French. When I asked her why she suddenly felt the urge, she said because Anthony was going to French school (his mother's choice, one I fully respect), and Mom wanted to converse with him. She has been in Quebec since 1960 but, beyond a few words, she didn't learn its official language. Although the argument can be made that she didn't exactly master English either. I applauded the effort, and tried my best to encourage her.

Philia, a non-profit volunteer organization that assists the elderly remnants of Park Extension's Greek community, the same group that set Mom up with older Greek-speaking widows who needed an interpreter at the doctor, was offering free French classes to the same women, almost all of whom were unilingual in their native tongue and knew only a few words or phrases in English or French. Mom was excited about the class and set the unrealistic goal of being perfectly fluent in French upon its completion six weeks later. While I knew she wasn't going to become an instant Catherine Deneuve, I was hoping she would at minimum take full advantage of the opportunity for personal growth and self-improvement. I should've known better. In the end her spoken French was more akin to Marcel Marceau's.

After her first few classes she presented me with her workbook, which was a Level 1 children's text, and asked me to do her homework for her; an assignment that consisted of verb conjugation exercises.

"What?" I said. "You want me to do it for you? I thought you wanted to learn. I'm not doing this. If you want me to help you I will, but no, I won't do it for you."

"You, you, you are *axristos*!" (Good for nothing) she said as she instantly flew into a blind rage, grabbing the workbook from my hands and violently throwing it against a wall, yelling "*rhé*, stupid guy! I do so much for you and you can't do *thees* for me!"

Serves me right for being optimistic. I may be *axristos*, but at least I did my own schoolwork ... most of the time.

A few months later Mom came home from the Rossy on Jean-Talon with a cheap plastic picture frame. She quickly hung it on the living room wall. In it was her certificate from the French course. It made me wonder who ended up doing her homework and taking her exams. With closer scrutiny I discovered that it said "participant." Everyone it seems got the same document just for showing up on diploma day.

* * *

Being a lifelong poor athlete, my personal trophy case is embarrassingly bare. All I have is a small statuette I earned for being number one in a quarterly sales derby when I was in financial services. Although I beat out the next highest person by one single point on the last day, I was up against over one hundred and fifty other people, so victory was no small task, and I readily admit that said triumph was more fortuitous than anything else; it could just as easily have gone the other way had the tournament lasted another day or two.

What I consider my greatest prizes are my diplomas, which take up a good portion of my office wall. While not competitive awards they are, for me, a consistently average student who didn't care much for academics, noteworthy achievements. I must clarify that, while my high school diploma says "Outremont High School," I did not officially graduate from that institution, having flunked out of Grade 11. I had to go to night school at The High School of Montreal to finish my studies a semester later, but I was not sent any new documents after earning my credits. So it is semi-truthful: I am a high school graduate, just not from the high school on the parchment.

When I was a kid the federal government had a program (that ended in 2001 and was revived some years later) called "ParticipACTION" (I guess it was intended as a combination of "participation" and "action," something that sort of works in both French and English, or perhaps one of the people who came up with the program may have said "participate in some action" too quickly, like the guy who asked Paul McCartney to pass the salt and pepper and inadvertently created "Sgt. Pepper"), and the Canada Fitness Award Program, which was intended to promote physical fitness among young people. They ran television and radio public service ads that featured Canadian "celebrities" (i.e. an actor vaguely familiar because they did a guest spot on *The Beachcombers* or were in a Canadian movie no one outside of their family saw) and highlighted the program's logo, a three-section swirl that was supposed to symbolize a person running, I guess? I don't know.

One summer day when I was about nine my brother and I were walking up Stuart Avenue headed for the Dairy Queen (for soft ice cream, not drugs, which were sold there as well; not by the employees but by Park Ex denizens in the parking lot) when a lean and energetic Asian kid on a bicycle blew past us and said "hi, Peter!" to my brother. The young man in question wore athletic shorts and a blue Adidas jacket with three yellow stripes down the sleeves, which was in style at the time. Stitched onto the back was a black and gold patch that had three small maple leaves below it in gold, silver, and bronze.

"You know him?" I asked.

"Yeah," Peter said, "that's Benson Fong. He's a kid in my class."

"What's that patch on his jacket? I've seen them before, but not like that."

"We do these tests in gym class. You'll probably do it next year. Depending on how in-shape you are you could get gold, silver, or bronze, like in the Olympics. The one he has? That's higher than gold. He was the only kid in all of Barclay to get that … yeah Benson, he's a really good athlete. I got a silver myself."

"How come I didn't see it? Don't you want Mom to sew it … ?"

"Ahh, I don't give a shit about that," he said with a wave.

Barclay Elementary School, for reasons unexplained, changed gym teachers annually. September that year was no exception: We had a new instructor for P.E., and the first thing we did was the Canada Fitness Award trials.

Each student was given a card with their name and classroom number on it, as well as their gender, date of birth, and various other stats. The program consisted of a series of physical challenges that tested our fitness level, like how many sit-ups we could do in an allotted time, speed and distance running, and the like. After each task we filled out our cards and at the end of class gave them back to the teacher. It took a few weeks to complete, then I forgot about the whole thing.

At the end of the school year the gym teacher came to our class and in a mini-ceremony handed out the patches. There were several golds issued and a few more silvers, but the majority had attained bronze. Six of us, including myself, got nothing but participant stickers. Truthfully I didn't really care. But what exactly were we expected to do with the stickers? Put them on our bikes or schoolbags? Or our binders? Who would want to advertise to bullies that we couldn't make the minimal fitness requirements? Why not just hang a sign on our back that says: "Come and get your free lunch here!"

The next year we had a strict, drill-sergeant gym teacher. He looked like he was cut from stone; a mean and no-nonsense hoser with a bushy brown mustache. We quickly learned not to screw around in his class. If anyone talked out of turn or otherwise acted out or misbehaved, he would subject us to a series of burpees, a punishing callisthenic where one begins in a standing position, does a squat, puts their hands on the floor, extends their legs, retracts their legs, and stands up again. It was not uncommon for him to force us to do seventy-five in a row. Grade 5 was when the boys and girls at Barclay had separate P.E., with the other half of the class being Grade 6ers, who were one year older, stronger, and faster than we were. I wondered if the sadistic asshole did the same thing to the girls' class with regard to burpees. I got my answer the next year in Grade 6 when we had a series of assemblies in the gymnasium where various area high schools delivered their pitch to potential new pupils. During one of the Q & A sessions, a girl put up her hand and asked the vice principal of Malcolm Campbell High School if their P.E. instructor gave out burpees as a punishment, which drew a huge round of laughter among the students; all this with the gym teacher in attendance.

The Sadist was a bully as well. There was an overweight kid in the Grade 6 class named Billy K. He had come over in what I called "The Algonquin Invasion" when Algonquin Elementary School in the neighbouring Town of Mount Royal converted to French and the surplus students were transferred to Barclay. He was a bit of a wise guy, getting us multiple sessions of burpees during the school year. Once in front of the whole class the gym teacher said to Billy K. that he was the worst case of obesity he had seen in his life. If that bothered Billy K., he didn't show it. In fact, the budding anarchist wore it as a badge of honour.

When we had the fitness trials that year, the Sadist spread them out over several months, and like previously, we were given our patches in May, except he did not bother coming to the class the way the last guy did. They were given to our regular classroom teacher and she handed them out. Now there were more golds and silvers than the previous year, and only two students didn't get anything: myself and a girl named Soula.

After school, I heard it from the rest of the class, taunted for not being able to get at least a bronze, which truth be told was actually not all that difficult to achieve. Soula, oddly enough, was left alone.

I saw Billy K. in the schoolyard with his buddies that afternoon. They were comparing patches. Billy K. somehow managed to score a bronze. I was floored!

How the hell did he get a bronze? He couldn't even run! He broke out in a sweat just standing still and breathing.

I confronted him and asked how a fat lazy guy like him was able to get a patch.

He replied: "*Rhé*, stupid," (I assumed he called me that because he was angry. I called him fat and lazy in front of his friends, as if I was divulging a secret), "the teacher doesn't check the names and stats on the cards. You can fill out whatever you want, *malaka*!"

The Canada Fitness people had naively and foolishly believed that the honour system was the way to go. They had failed to anticipate that they could be bamboozled by grade schoolers.

I was determined not to be left out and laughed at again, so I started a rigorous and strenuous exercise and nutrition program that summer, and ... who am I fooling? That summer I went right back to the couch in front of the TV and spent my days sleeping in late and bumming around, occasionally riding bikes and thinking that was enough.

The next year the sadistic asshole was back and I fudged my results, adding reps to my sit-ups and so forth, all the while nervously worrying that I would be caught and sent to a gulag where I would be assigned infinite burpees for all eternity. I didn't know what the standards were, so I had no clue if I would get anything, but I was careful to fake at least plausible times and reps. But I didn't have to change most of my running stats. I was a good sprinter; as fast as anyone, quicker than most.

In May a manila envelope arrived again from Ottawa and like all the kids in my class I had attained a patch. A nice, "respectable" bronze.

I took it home and looked at it for a long time.

Should I ask Mom to sew it on my jacket? Should I even show it to my parents?

The reality started to sink in: It was an ill-gotten gain, a symbol of my failure to make a real, serious effort. The more I stared at it, the more it mocked me. It felt worse than the laughter of my peers. I became disgusted, shoving it in my desk drawer, and did not see it again until my early 20s when I cleaned out my old desk and ditched the wreck in favour of a computer-friendly one.

When I re-examined it as an adult I didn't feel any better. It was just a reminder of my lacklustre childhood and the rewards of dishonesty. I don't remember what I did with it or what happened to it, but I hope I don't come across the stupid thing again.

They didn't have the Canada Fitness Program in my high school. I was glad to be done with it, but I will not soon forget the great lesson it taught me: It's all right to be just a participant, as long as you try.

DEAD SHRIMP

My father didn't live with us full time until the early 70s. When he finally moved in permanently, or so he intended, we didn't have much. All of our furniture, curtains, and appliances were used, given to us for free or for almost nothing, and had a tendency to break down and come apart. My bed, just a steel frame with a box spring and mattress, was missing a leg. (Dad propped it up with phone books.) In time Dad sprung for some wooden posts, tacks, and a length of vinyl and made us a decent set of headboards. We didn't have a TV (Dad considered them too bourgeois) until an old black and white one was procured from someone who planned to toss in the trash. It was so solidly built it lasted until we threw it out years later, not once in need of repair, and replaced it with the epic Zenith System 3 console, our main source of entertainment for the next decade and a half.

What's more, we didn't go on vacations until the mid-70s. Holidays for most people in the Greek community consisted of summer-long treks back to Greece where they often stayed with relatives, an endeavour too extravagant for our family.

When we lived on Birnam Street one of our neighbours was a retired elderly *Anglaisis* couple my mom quickly befriended. She noticed that they were away each weekend and when she asked where they went she discovered they had a cottage in the country. Polite society dictated that an invitation be extended to us to go and one was offered, probably thinking Mom would say no, but desperate for a chance to go anywhere new she immediately replied: "When? How about this weekend?"

So the next time they went they brought me, Mom, and my brother along in their wood-panelled station wagon. Their cottage was small with two bedrooms. They were courteous and generous to us, but I had the feeling that they weren't too crazy about having guests, especially after they bought groceries and Mom only half-heartedly offered to pay for part of them. They took us to a lake where we could swim, and showed us around. One night while walking along a dirt road Mom noticed the trail broke off into another direction. When she asked what was along that path, the usually pleasant husband's face turned ugly as he said: "Don't go there! That's Indian land. Lousy, filthy Indians."

They brought us home on Sunday night. Mom didn't speak to them as much anymore after that.

A couple of years later we took a bus trip to Atlantic City. It was a charter arranged through a Greek community organization and we stayed at a guest house owned by fellow Greeks called the "Olympic Guest House." (Greeks name all their businesses after the Olympics or, for reasons that to this day I still have a tremendous amount of difficulty fully comprehending, whether it is a restaurant or dry cleaner or whatnot, either "New System" or "New Method.") We met the bus at the corner of L'Acadie and Jarry. A number of other families were there as well waiting with their suitcases. I was five years old at the time and thought that the bus came by there regularly like Montreal public transit to take people to New Jersey.

Atlantic City had not yet built all the casinos so it was more of a low-key, run-down vacation town. The whole time there we did not go more than two hundred meters from the beach, which was fine. It marked the first time I had been to the U.S., put my feet into salt water, and most importantly the first time I had seen my parents in an ocean. We had been to swimming areas before, but they were Quebec or Ontario lakes, ponds or rivers. The ocean was different. I could not see the other side; its vastness alone amazed me. The sandy shore appeared endless. Mom and Dad just dove into the water with reckless abandon. I was unsure what to do. I slowly waded in up to my waist, but the persistent waves were jarring and to a pre-kindergartener they were like tsunamis taller than Place Ville Marie. The fresh water beaches were not that way. At my feet were crabs and other sea life and I had no idea how to react to them. The first day was exploratory, but the next day I didn't go in any deeper while Peter started to get used to it all and have fun with other kids. I was still uncomfortable. Dad showed me how he floated on his back, a technique he learned in the navy as a means of surviving until being rescued should one fall overboard.

In the evening we would hit the long boardwalk. The first night a police patrol car pulled up to my parents. One of the officers was Black which to me was a new experience because at the time the Montreal Police Department was whiter than a Swedish snowstorm. They spoke to my parents for a few seconds then drove on. When I asked my father what they said, he told me the cops said that my mother should carry her purse with the strap cross body to prevent it from being snatched, and that it wasn't a good idea for Dad to have his jacket draped over his shoulders for the same reason.

The boardwalk reminded me of Belmont Park with all its games, rides, attractions, a mustachioed man with a hurdy-gurdy and trained monkey, and something I saw for the first time: miniature golf!

My father didn't like spending money on carnival games, but he eased up a bit and gave me quarters for things like slot machines that featured dancing ducks. (I didn't know at the time that they were "dancing" on a hotplate … but I had a feeling Dad did; in fact he appeared more amused by it than I was.) People were walking around with what was the latest craze, the "invisible dog," which was a stiff leash and collar that gave the impression one was walking a ghost canine. I asked Dad to buy me one, but he realized the frivolity of it and refused. When I persisted, he exclaimed: "*Yeti tôh thelis efôh*! *Einai malakias*" (Why do you want that? It's … stupid). He thought the mini golf was just as asinine, but at least he took us there and we all had a blast.

By day four I had still made no progress in learning to swim so my impatient father decided to take matters into his own hands. He scooped me up despite my objections and started walking into the sea. He meant well and was merely trying to show me that there was nothing to fear, but all it did was cause me to panic. My feet could not touch the bottom and I was horribly uncomfortable. Looking back on it now, my father was five-foot-six and I was taller than him by the time I had reached thirteen, so the water we were in would not come up to my armpits today, but at the time I was scared witless. Not that I felt Dad would purposely drown me, just that he didn't take the gravity of my dilemma seriously and might drop me thinking I would suddenly learn to tread water. I screamed and yelled and struggled but he ignored my pleas and held me even tighter. To make matters worse he laughed as if how I felt was meaningless to him. After what felt like an eternity we returned to the shore and he let me go. I ran straight to our towels on the beach and did not go back to the water again the rest of the day, and for the remainder of the trip I kept an eye on him to make sure he couldn't do that again. What was intended as my first swimming lesson had only succeeded in making me more fearful of the deep blue ocean.

In 1978 we took a family trip to Florida. We drove down and stayed with a friend of my father's whose family was away for the summer in Greece. (I often wonder where people who live in places others go to for holidays went for vacations themselves ... I mean, do people in Las Vegas go somewhere like Peoria just to experience banality? Would that be fun for them?)

When we went to the beach my brother took to the ocean with swim goggles, a small red and white inner tube, and a set of flippers. He spent all day paddling with his arms and legs going back and forth across the surf. Each day he disencumbered himself of his accessories; the inner tube, the goggles, and finally the flippers were gone. He taught himself to swim by the end of the vacation. As for me, Dad did the same thing he did in Atlantic City, but this time it was daily. I learned only to dread the beach, and was relieved on the days we went to the Miami Seaquarium, ("Seaquarium?" Really? Even back then it felt like a lame, phony, fake, made-up word like "spork"), and Walt Disney World, which was lame, phony and fake, too. What I remember most about our trip to the "Magic Kingdom" was that I could not find one single souvenir keychain or licence plate with the name "Andreas" on it. They had every name but mine. I had to settle for a leather octagon keychain that said "Andy," which to this day I hate to be called. Peter of course found one that said "Peter."

On what was our final day in the Sunshine State I did not want to go to the beach. I was defiant but my parents dragged me there. When we arrived I noticed people fishing at one of the piers.

Fishing! I thought. *A possible salvation.*

I hadn't been fishing before and was curious to see what it was like.

I asked if I could go, but Dad said no, because it was stupid. And he had a point. What would we do with the fish we caught? He was a practical man and did not understand the concept of "catch and release." For him fishing meant you ate what you caught; it was only polite. In his eyes it would be like going hunting, shooting a bird or rabbit, resuscitating it, healing its wounds, and returning it to the wild.

I insisted and Mom made Dad take me.

"Fine," he said, grabbing my hand and pulling me along, "let's *falking* go!"

I thought my folks would let me fish alone. Dad wanted to enjoy what would be his last day at an ocean for a while, and it was not my intention to ruin it for him. I just didn't want to get dragged out into the sea and possibly drowned. I had numerous plans for my life and no desire to die that day.

There was a booth on the pier where they rented rods and other fishing equipment. Dad asked the attendant how much it was for the gear and when told the hourly rate he said "*salababeech*!" and asked for one rod for one hour.

"Don't you want one too?" I said.

"I do not want to *feesh*. You want to do *thees*!" he grumbled. Then Dad asked: "What *eez thee tseepest* bait?"

The attendant pulled out an envelope full of what looked like small, slimy, grey insects and plopped it on the counter.

"Dead shrimp. One dollar," he said.

Dead shrimp? I wondered. *Do they also have the option of live shrimp, sick shrimp, or shrimp on life support? Had they arrived at his booth alive or dying, and what exactly was their cause of death?*

When I asked Dad to speculate as to what was the cause of the shrimps' ultimate demise, he replied: "*Mee lais malakias*!" (Don't say ... stupidities).

Dad begrudgingly took me to a spot on the pier where the water was deep and taught me how to bait a hook and cast off. He did not appear to enjoy the experience one bit and keep looking longingly at the beach, yearning to swim in the beautiful Atlantic one more time.

I leaned over the pier and saw some large fish swimming about, but for them, the dead shrimp must have been unappetizing.

Were they turned off by the possible disease that killed the shrimp?

I asked Dad if he could get the live shrimp, suggesting it might work better.

"*Stamata nah lehss malakias*!" (Stop saying ... stupidities) was his quick reply.

Much smaller fish were nibbling away at my hook, but we failed to catch a thing and the moment the hour was up Dad collected our gear and practically threw it at the attendant as he grabbed my hand and hurried us back to the beach where he immediately took off his shirt and baby blue polyester Bermuda shorts and made a B-line for the ocean. His deeply tanned, hair-covered, Speedo-clad body was soon crashing the surf. I watched him come up floating with a big smile on his face, especially as my self-taught brother casually and confidently swam past him.

The next three family vacations were in Cape Cod. We often went there with my mother's sister and her family ... like most Greeks they were drawn to the ocean and were all natural swimmers who didn't irrationally dread the sea. By then I had grown large enough that Dad could not easily muscle me into the surf. I had taken to wading in up to my chest and floating with the waves, but that was about it and for the most part my cousins didn't give me too hard a time about that.

Once when we were all wading together one of my cousins spotted a jellyfish. We wasted no time getting out of there. We reported it to my mom upon reaching the shore, and without hesitation she grabbed a diving mask, asked us to point out where it was, and instructed us to dig a hole in the sand for her. She confidently waded in, found the interloper, carefully fished it out using the diving mask, brought it ashore, dropped it into the newly dug "grave," and told us to bury the beast. My mother, who grew up poor and rarely made it to the beach as a child, knew just what to do and had no fear of the sea creature that could have seriously hurt her.

To this day the memories of Dad's "swimming lessons" still haunt me. (He probably thought a technique similar to the one he used to teach me to ride a bicycle would work in water.) With the help and encouragement of my smooth and wily lifelong friend The Weasel, himself an avid swimmer, I have since learned to be more comfortable at the beach, tread water without looking like too big a fool who is about to drown (more like a fancy dog paddle, but I'll take it), and even swim a bit, but the unease remains and I still don't go in water deeper than my neck. If my feet can't touch the bottom I sometimes suffer a panic attack, even in a swimming pool. And I wear a life vest when I am in a canoe, kayak, or rowboat, although that is what one is supposed to do anyway. My phobia nearly ruined an expensive vacation I took to the Dominican Republic with a girlfriend who was not just an enthusiastic beachgoer, but a certified lifeguard to boot.

When I'm at a beach I stare out at the wide, blue expanse and I can't help but ponder how I would have progressed if simply left to my own devices.

MR. BERTON

At the elementary level, the Protestant School Board of Greater Montreal offered three possible report card grades. The best you could get is a "C" for "Commendable." If you passed and did okay, you received an "S" for "Satisfactory." If you failed a course, you were branded with the dreaded "HD" for "Has Difficulty." For the most part, my report card was a sea of S's with a peppering of C's. My father would scan the yellow, three-way folded, hand-written document and before signing it would proclaim in his thick accent with great shame, "Why you no have more *coh-mmendable*? You should have more *coh-mmendable*!" My brother Peter often had more C's than I did. (My father didn't know the exact English definition of "Commendable" or "Satisfactory" or even "Has Difficulty," he just knew where they ranked.)

"More *coh-mmendable*!" he would exclaim, waving the report card in my face. One year he told me that if I attained sixteen "*coh-mmendable*" he would, in what I felt was a breach of his communist principles, reward me with a new ten-speed bicycle from the Canadian Tire on L'Acadie and Sauvé.

Elementary school was relatively easy for the first three grades. Most of what we did would involve childish games and simple math. Art was fun (one of my few consistent C's, and it of course would be the one subject my father didn't give a shit about), and there was relatively little pressure on the kids to perform academically. That changed in Grade 4. Playtime was over.

The curriculum ratcheted a few notches higher and we were expected to be more mature and serious, and I did not step up my game. On top of that it was around the time my parents' marriage, flawed and tenuous, began to disintegrate, making home life a stressful and monstrous distraction. My teacher that year was Mrs. Sousa, a relatively young but experienced teacher who would often lose her shit and shout at the class "I am *FURIOUS*!" when she got upset. It was bad enough I had to deal with all the yelling at home, but school, which until then was somewhat of a sanctuary, was now pressing me and I was left with nowhere to turn.

I became wary of Mrs. Sousa when she was chastising a student I had known since kindergarten. He was a good kid, but not impressive academically or intellectually. She was letting him have it for his sub-par math skills, trying to emphasize how important it was for his future. When she asked what he wanted to do for a living when he grew up, he said sheepishly, "I want to be an astronaut."

"Astronaut!?! Really!?! An astronaut!?!" she said, appalled by the very notion. "Astronauts begin as test pilots! And all pilots have to be good at math. You are pathetic at math! You'll never be a pilot, let alone an astronaut! Get that silly idea out of your head!"

I sat silently as I witnessed that soul-crushing moment. The kid lowered his head and slinked off. I could not understand what the harm would've been to let him keep his ambition. He would get older and the astronaut dream would melt away before he mailed a job application to NASA.

Mrs. Sousa came off as a little cold and was not one to get friendly or talk personally with the students the way other elementary teachers did. When she started the school year she wore mostly tight, I mean excessively tight, almost inappropriately tight, sweaters to class, displaying her flat stomach, curvy figure, and impressive rack. By the end of the year, she cut her long, brown wavy hair short and started sporting muumuus. It wasn't until the last day of class that one of the girls asked if she were pregnant, and Mrs. Sousa confessed she was.

Why didn't she share the good news? I thought. *Did she think so little of us?* (Maybe she was concerned about jinxing it and having a miscarriage, but by the end of the school year she looked about ready to pop. Did she think we were morons and wouldn't notice?)

Midway through Grade 4 we were assigned a science project to complete, and I put it off until a specific weekend just before it was due. Unluckily for me on that Saturday my parents got into what remains the worst argument they'd had to date. It was so distressing that I spent the weekend in the tiny room I shared with my brother, lying on my bed upset beyond words over what was transpiring in our home. I was unable to complete my work and handed it in half-done. I was too ashamed to tell Mrs. Sousa why. Fortunately for me, some other students did the same, although I don't know if their parents went at it as well.

Mrs. Sousa was "furious" again, but she did not single out any students except for George R., our resident nerd, who not only completed the project but did an exceptional job. She told the class we should all be more like him, which I guess was worse than having a finger pointed at you and told you sucked because all the other students began to resent him. That Christmas I brought home a report card that contained my first and only "HD." My father acted as though the world had come to an end. He demanded to know why, and I couldn't tell him it was because he and Mom had had a row and a half and it wounded me so much I couldn't function. He wouldn't have understood. And he didn't get over the "HD" or let me forget that my grades somehow ruined *his* life, oblivious to what their carrying on did to me.

Despite the "HD" I passed Grade 4 and moved on to the 5th Grade. We had no idea which teachers we were getting until we showed up at school on the first Tuesday after Labour Day. That year my assigned educator was Mrs. Randstad, who was labelled with the most unfortunate nickname of "The Rodent." She had a reputation for being tough and mean. I thought I was in for another difficult year.

The Grade 5 moment that stands out in my mind was the time I had failed to do a homework assignment (yet another nightmarish fight between my parents) and as punishment she made me sit outside the classroom to complete it as the rest of the class had an art session. After a while my pencil became dull, so I just sauntered into the class and swaggered up to the large crank sharpener, used it, and walked right out without saying a word, while the whole room stopped what they were doing and watched me. Protocol required that I asked permission to do so, but I was angry and full of attitude because I hated missing art class, which throughout Barclay was the highlight of my week.

What did Mrs. Randstad do?

She took a chair and sat with me outside the class.

Did she yell at me? Humiliate me? Put me in my place? That's what I was braced for.

No. She looked me in the eye and talked calmly and directly, not condescending, and treated me with respect and dignity. She took the time to explain why what I did was wrong, and said that she knew I was intelligent and capable of doing better. I was shocked.

Years later The Weasel's then-girlfriend now wife was studying to be a teacher at McGill University. I was pleased to discover that Mrs. Randstad was one of her instructors; my first impression of the veteran educator could not have been more wrong. Not only was she the best teacher I had at Barclay, but she still ranks among the best I had in my life. Sure, she assigned tons of homework, but she spent time helping students who were having trouble as well. She didn't diminish anyone in the class. She talked about her home life, her golden retriever, and her husband. And occasionally she would bake us a carrot cake or cookies.

Grade 5 was my best year academically at Barclay, and while I had what was for me a record number of C's, I did not achieve the coveted sixteen and fell short of earning a new bicycle. Truth be known, Dad probably forgot about his promise because he didn't mention it again.

My Grade 6 teacher was Mr. Berton, a chubby, thirtysomething, blue-eyed, blonde-haired West Islander with a rapidly retreating hairline and two gold front teeth. He was wearing a white shirt without a tie, unbuttoned at the collar, and a cheap sports coat. I looked at him and thought that this year was going to be a breeze.

Once again my first impressions were horrifically wrong.

Mr. Berton was new to Barclay. He had transferred from a school in the East End that was closing due to declining enrollment. (Quebec language protection laws passed in the 70s halted English enrollment for immigrant children whose parents were not educated in English and so numerous institutions were closed or switched to French.)

Mr. Berton was a bachelor, blowhard, and bookworm who'd often bore the class to tears with long, pretentious talks he would call "day-end speeches" where he would review the homework assignments and make other comments. His teaching style did not match those of the other Barclay long-termers. For example, he didn't run off stencils for tests. I don't know if he didn't know how to use the stencil machine or he didn't like the smell of the ink or was just plain lazy but for exams he would hand out blank lined sheets and write the questions or math problems on the blackboard or read them out to us. Again I don't know if it was laziness or what, but he would not even bother to mark the tests himself. He would have us hand our papers to the person behind us, and read the answers aloud while we graded them. Then the part I hated the most: He would call out students' names, and we, in front of the whole class, read out loud how we did. He'd sometimes admonish a student for poor efforts and single out individuals for scorn when they got answers wrong. He once pointed out to the class that I was the worst speller he'd seen in his career. (Yeah, well, fuk yoo, azzhol!)

He was unaware that I was on the spectrum, which I now believe to be the cause of my inability to spell at a Grade 6 level. (I myself was guilty of being equally ignorant of that fact at the time.) But he was an experienced professional educator and should have known something was up. He couldn't spot that I was unlike my classmates? Was he not trained to look out for possible learning disabilities? What did he do? He ridiculed me rather than offer any constructive or useful instruction on how to improve. One time he told the class that he had discussed me with the school's vice principal, wondering how a student who seemed so bright got such poor grades. According to Mr. Berton, they then looked up my grades, discovering that in the past my marks had been consistently unremarkable. Did it not occur to them that maybe I didn't fit in with the traditional education system, and perhaps I could've prospered at some kind of alternative school or specialized education? (But when I think about it now, back then Quebec "specialized" education would have meant a school where they'd teach me to finger-paint and make me wear an electrified helmet that would shock me if I misbehaved, so perhaps I was better off at Barclay after all.)

What I did like about him was that in class we played a trivia game called *Reach for the Top*, based on the popular CBC TV show where teams of high school students faced off against each other. (When I got to high school I wanted to try out for the team, but as soon as I was old enough the show was cancelled. I guess *Reach for the Top* wasn't quite as popular as I thought. I still have a feeling that was done to purposely rob me of my chance to shine.)

During one game Mr. Berton asked, "Who killed Kennedy?"

My hand shot up.

"Andreas," he said.

"Sirhan Sirhan," the first name that, in my anxious state, came to mind because he had been in the news recently, trying unsuccessfully to get paroled for assassinating *Robert* Kennedy.

"Not the answer I wanted, but I was not specific. One point for that team. I meant who killed *John F.* Kennedy?"

My hand shot up again.

"Andreas," he said.

"Lee Harvey Oswald," I said, having settled down.

"Correct, one more point for that team. Now, who killed Oswald?"

Once again my hand shot up.

"Andreas," he said.

"Jack Ruby."

"Correct, one more point for Andreas' team."

Before the next question, I heard one boy whisper faintly to another, "The fuckin' guy."

That was the moment I realized my fellow students were unimpressed with my knowledge. I was once selected by Mr. Berton as MVP of the tournament and my teams often did well. I thought my abilities would earn their respect. Instead they labelled me "weird" and I became an outcast. It's not like I bragged about it, or rubbed the losing team's face in it. If I had walked across the St. Lawrence River, my classmates would point, laugh, and say, "Look at Andreas! He can't swim!" Which I actually can't, but that's not my point. (There was a kid in the class named Achilles whose trivial knowledge rivalled my own, but he garnered way more esteem from the others, especially Mr. Berton, than I did, likely due to the fact that he was a honours student whose grades were consistently among the highest, or possibly it was his quiet, polite, and decidedly "unweird" demeanour.)

* * *

And it wouldn't be the last time. Years later I had the honor of attending film classes at university with a world-renowned film critic and historian named Marc Gervais. I'd often correct him in class when he'd get a detail wrong, something I regretted after I found out decades later that in his 80s he had Alzheimer's. I wasn't trying to show him up or be a jerk. It just irks me when people don't have their facts straight. I have since learned to be more discreet, but at the time the proper social skills eluded me. Marc would mention a scene from a movie and I would say, "No, that was *The Life and Times of Judge Roy Bean*" and not the picture he was talking about. He didn't get angry with me (he was a Jesuit Priest and perhaps that taught him humility, or maybe he just didn't mind ... I didn't speak to him about it), and took it all in stride. We became good friends.

We were studying westerns, especially the films of legendary Hollywood director John Ford, that semester. One night we would see the movie, and the next night we would discuss it. This was before digital DVDs and streaming, so Marc had a T.A. run a projector in the lecture class and we would do scene analysis. The day after we screened *The Oxbow Incident* (directed by William "Wild Bill" Wellman) we were deconstructing a scene in which a housekeeper, who had a small part in the film, shows a group of men to her employer's parlour. After the discussion, the T.A. was moving on to the next scene when I piped up.

"Hey, Marc? Y'know who played the housekeeper, there? It's Margaret Hamilton. She played the Wicked Witch of the West in *The Wizard of Oz*!"

Marc looked baffled. I don't know if he was unsure it was her, or just confused as to why I or anyone would care. But the rest of the class insisted they run the scene again; they wanted to see her without the green makeup. There was a chorus of "oohs" as they replayed it. Probably because I had already established myself as an uncool, unhip, and unpopular misfit within the film program, I once again failed to impress my classmates.

Strangely enough it was Mr. Berton who suggested that I watch certain TV shows, like *Sneak Previews* on PBS with Gene Siskel and Roger Ebert, which ignited my lifelong love affair with the cinema, thus leading me to the aforementioned film school.

* * *

Grade 6 went awry for me around midyear. That was when I became Mr. Berton's favourite target. One day in class he had students take turns reading from a story in one of our textbooks. When I was up, I mistakenly said "speared" instead of "spread" with regards to putting butter on toast with a knife, which drew a few snickers from my fellow students. I quickly corrected myself, but Mr. Berton started mocking me in front of my classmates. It lasted the whole afternoon, and at the end of the school day, he admitted that hearing me say that gave him an incurable case of the giggles. But it didn't stop that day. The next morning Mr. Berton continued, and some of the kids joined him; he did nothing to discourage them. Quite the opposite; he even complimented their "wit" like a cheerleader.

What bothered me the most was that I had a crush on a girl who sat adjacent to me, named Stella. She was petite and cute, with short reddish-brown pixie hair; rocking the Pat Benatar look, which was all the rage back then. Gym class in Grade 6 was separate for boys and girls, but I saw her once in her gym uniform: leg warmers and leotards, with a white sweatband around her temples, thus capturing the 80s Olivia Newton-John "Let's Get Physical" look, also popular at that time. All she needed was to wear lace like Stevie Nicks and she would hit the trifecta, but that didn't matter because she had already set my twelve-year-old heart aflutter. Stella joined with the others and picked on me; my heart went from "afluttering" to "aflopping," sinking slowly and painfully like a torpedoed battleship upon realizing she saw me as a laughingstock.

Stella wasn't interested in me anyway. She, like most of the girls, liked Petros, another one of those who came to Barclay in the "Algonquin Invasion." He had thick, wavy, light-brown hair with eyes to match, insane cheekbones, and was athletic, although his principal advantage was that he was a year older than the rest of us because he failed Grade 4 and had already started puberty. It was the blonde-haired and blue-eyed Taylors who in turn caught his eye. The Taylor twins, Mary-Anne and Mary-Rose (who despite their names and complexion were actually Greek), lived upstairs from the restaurant their father owned on the corner of Jean-Talon and Stuart. They were both athletic, and today I'd say had a Linda Hamilton sort of vibe (who by the way has an identical twin, too). They hung around with Petros in what was an interesting threesome. Because the girls lived on my street I would occasionally see them together, although after leaving Barclay I didn't happen across any of them again.

Later that year the class started learning to debate. For one session the question was, "Is Canada better than the U.S.A.?" Stella had pros, and when she stood up to make her case, she simply listed off terrible things about America. One of her points was a titbit that I imagined she picked up from an adult relative overheard at some family gathering: "America has Black people who get drunk every night and live on the street in cardboard boxes," a statement that drew some awkward giggles from our classmates, and a shocked, prolonged gasp from me. She didn't seem so cute anymore.

Mr. Berton, when giving his post-debate evaluation, ignored the statement, which I found perplexing: I had once said that I thought cows were ugly, and he gave me an hour-long scolding in front of the whole class about how we should not judge people by their appearance, but a white-hooded Stella gets a "get out of jail free" card?

It didn't occur to take what Mr. Berton did to me to my parents or the Principal. Back then it was as though students had little or no recourse in such matters. When I told my parents that the Greek school teacher beat me with a ruler, their response was to say I likely did something to deserve it. The school was like a prison yard where the students were expected to fend for themselves with little to no protection from authority figures. Even if you reported a fellow student as being abusive, most teachers would look at you as if you were a loser for doing so and encourage you to stand up for yourself, essentially implying that violence was the best way to resolve the issue. And if you were outnumbered? Starting or joining a gang was the direction they were pushing us. In my time at Barclay I was rarely bullied by just one kid. It was usually a group. (When they were by themselves I was more often than not left alone.) What lessons were we being taught? Adults have the use of police and lawyers if someone threatens them with violence or tries to rob or cheat them. Have you heard of a lawyer or policeman saying, "That guy stole your car? Why are you bothering me? Get a baseball bat and get your car back, wimp!"? Why do adults have more rights than children? Why does the rule of law end in the schoolyard? And if you told on anyone you were called a "rat" or a "snitch," both of which are inaccurate. (For the record, a "rat" is someone who engages in illicit activity and when they get caught tells on their cohorts to save their skin; a "snitch" is a person who sticks their nose in the illegal business of others and then tells the authorities for their personal gain.)

But what is one to do if their bully is a teacher? What was my recourse? Could I win? Would anyone believe me?

After a few days of almost constant teasing (even one of my cousins, who was in my Grade 6 class with me, had mercilessly joined the chorus), I had had enough. Mr. Berton started on me again, and I lost it. I stood up defiantly and cursed him in front of the class, telling him that he could stick his sarcasm (even though the humour he was employing was technically not sarcasm) up his fat, white … you can figure out what I said. A hush fell upon the room. Mr. Berton turned deadly serious. I could tell he was upset; his face went from pasty white to a pinkish, swine-like off-white.

"Andreas!" he said, "See me after school!"

At 3 pm class was dismissed, and I stayed behind.

"You were quite rude," he said to me.

I tried to stand my ground without sounding like a whiner. I was unsuccessful.

"Well, what about what you're doing? Is that polite? The other kids are laughing at me all the time! I can't take it anymore!"

"Okay, Andreas. A joke is a joke but you were rude just there. And if they make fun of you, you should stand up for yourself."

I couldn't believe what I was hearing. I had just stood up to my main bully and had to stay after school for it and miss *The Alan Thicke Show*, which aired on CFCF-12 at 3 pm on weekdays at the time, for my efforts. I didn't even get an apology from him.

"It's not a joke to me. I'm not laughing. It's no fun for me," I said. "I should tell my parents …"

"Nobody likes a tattle-tale, Andreas," he said. I didn't realize at the time that I had hit a nerve and he knew that if I spoke up he could potentially get into serious trouble; if I did I could've leveraged it to my advantage.

Mr. Berton gathered himself, sighed, and said, "I will stop if you quit being such a baby about this. And I'll tell the others to stop as well," as if he were doing me a favour.

I wanted to say to his face, "Sorry to spoil your fun, you fat ugly whitey!" but instead I said I was appreciative and he let me go. It was a miniscule victory for me and I figured this was the most I would get from him. I just wanted the whole stupid thing to be over.

For a while he stopped, although he reneged on his promise to tell my classmates to leave me alone. Then there was the incident with Mr. Law.

Mr. Law was the Vice Principal at Barclay. He was something of an anachronism: A tall, pear-shaped middle-aged man who wore sweater vests and a pair of horn-rimmed glasses. His haircut was out of date by decades with little to no hair on the sides and parted down the middle. He looked like a rock & roll-hating former marine dad from a movie that took place in the 50s. The most no-nonsense tight-ass I'd come across in my life; one of those "you are not here to have fun! You are here to *learn*!" types. The entire student body despised him.

The Greek Community rented Barclay for Greek school on Saturdays. The students used our classroom and desks and would often vandalize or steal our stuff. We complained to Mr. Berton, who in turn complained to the administration. Sick of hearing our gripes, Mr. Law stormed into our classroom accompanied by the school's custodian. Right in front of us he told Mr. Berton not to bellyache about it again, saying that the students had a "vivid imagination" and that the custodian said there were no Greek classes held in our room that Saturday, even though there were Greek letters written on our blackboard, erased but still lightly visible. Mr. Berton was pissed about being humiliated in front of his class by a superior, so of course he started to pick on me again as though our previous conversation hadn't happened. I really hope it made him feel better.

Mr. Berton, for reasons unexplained, had a problem with Hollywood celebrities like Sylvester Stallone (he often bragged that he was taller than the star of *Rocky*) and Tom Selleck, whose show *Magnum, P.I.* was all the rage in the early 80s. Mr. Berton would mock him in class because he didn't like the size of his nose, or something like that, and not once or twice. It was an obsession with him. Moreover, he had disdain for Lee Majors, calling him a "fat, old ex-football player who probably couldn't run up a flight of stairs," as if the rotund and doughy Mr. Berton himself was the model of physical fitness.

"Tom Selleck was in a cigarette commercial," he would say, "and some producer in Hollywood saw it and thought he looked like a detective. That's why he's on TV now." One day he picked on Selleck so much that one of the girls in the class started to cry. Then Mr. Berton started ridiculing her. (I wasn't the only student he picked on, just his favourite and most common target.)

Mr. Berton liked to brag to the class when he had a date. He'd say to us, "I have an engagement tonight," with a devilish and immeasurably inappropriate grin, which to me meant he bought new binoculars to spy on whatever poor, unfortunate woman he was stalking.

In the spring we took a class trip to Ottawa. We visited the Canada Science and Technology Museum, renowned for its "Crazy Kitchen" (a room with a slanted floor that makes one stand awkwardly, leaning like the Tower of Pisa). In the new technology section, there was a display that had a microphone where you can record a message and it would be played back a few seconds later. I know it seems lame now, but in 1982 it was cutting-edge. Mr. Berton called me over to listen to what he had just recorded. When I did and the playback began, it was a statement about "spearing toast." I walked away in disgust as he said, "C'mon, don't be like that! You baby!"

When our tour bus arrived at Parliament Hill we walked around the back of the building, past the library. One of the kids noticed the steep, high drop-off (well duh, it's called Parliament *Hill* for a reason) and began hawking loogies over the edge. Within a matter of minutes we all started doing the same. Mr. Berton was standing there enjoying the view when Steve R., a small, sort of spazzy kid, decided to give it a try. Steve R. lived on Ball Avenue just a block over from the school and was well-known not for something he had done, but because his father, a Greek immigrant just like my dad, was a mechanic who drove a tricked-out Trans Am that had a large, curvy wing on the back and a tacky, glittery, sparkly paint job, which was briefly considered cool in the Disco-era 70s. That car was legendary in Park Extension.

Instead of mustering a giant spit gob in his mouth, leaning over, and expectorating it slowly to see it drop, Steve R. fired off a clumsy spray in all directions. I was out of range, but Mr. Berton got it full force, right in his round, pale mug.

"Steve!" he said. "You spit in my face!"

All the kids started laughing uncontrollably, led by me. And I did not stop all day.

Mr. Berton was visibly angry as he wiped his cheeks and forehead with a handkerchief. It must have been a strong level of embarrassment for him because his face bypassed pink and went straight to a deep red; he looked like a big tomato. He marched away, muttering to himself: "I can't believe he spit in my face."

Later that day I bought Steve R. a Coke.

"Why are you giving me this?" he said.

"Oh… no reason," I said with a broad grin. "No reason at all."

HOT DOG

In the autumn of 2020 my partner Kay and I rented a house in her hometown, nestled in the Laurentian Mountains, for a few months. She needed to get away from the raging COVID-19 pandemic to concentrate on her dissertation. I came up for weekends and two weeks in mid-October.

We spent most afternoons taking long constitutionals up and down various roads and paths, like the Zen-inducing Aerobic Corridor, which her stepfather helped create. Kay would relate to me various anecdotes of her youth in a small town when we encountered places like her old elementary school or a property where her aunt, uncle, and cousins had lived for years.

One pleasant afternoon we took a long sojourn up the steep and scenic Bennett Road. I huffed and gasped my way, dragging my sumo-like frame as best I could towards the summit. Kay of course just loped along with the endurance, confidence, and skill of a mountain goat; little did I know a piece of my own Laurentian history would soon surface.

By midafternoon, we arrived at the ski hill, the town's main tourist attraction now that Le Studio had not only ceased operation and partially burned down, but was razed as well, so that all that was left was a small memorial to Rush's *Signals* album, placed there by obsessive fans.

We were greeted by a mosaic of green, yellow, brown, and red-leaved trees covering the vast hills under a sunny sky. The expanse was devoid of other people because it was pre-season, giving it a post-apocalyptic atmosphere.

I stood in silence and looked around.

That was the hill. That was the chalet. This was the place.

I had been there before …

***

Growing up in the city I didn't know much about skiing, even though it was a large part of winter tourism in Quebec. Starting in the late Fall, Guy Thibaudeau would appear at the end of CFCF's *Pulse* news program and read out ski conditions in the Laurentian, Quebec City, and Eastern Township regions, as well as across the border in Vermont. Occasionally I'd see billboards in the city with slogans like "*Skier le fun*" (French that probably gave the *OQLF* headaches, and if it didn't it should have), advertising certain hills and resorts. But skiing remained to me the domain of rich WASPs from TMR or Westmount with names like Brad, Skippy, Chad, or Chip who punctuated their sentences with words like "dude," "totally," and "awesome."

When I was young, one of my way-older cousins came by for a visit. His arm was in a sling. It turned out he had a new girlfriend who liked skiing, and he lied to her and said he loved to do it as well. (I guess she failed to question how someone born and raised in Greece loved winter sports.) So he hit the slopes with her and the damn fool injured himself. Goes without saying the relationship didn't last.

Years later I came home from elementary school to find my brother stretched out on the living room couch, complaining of soreness. When I asked what happened he told me that his high school had a ski trip and he had just returned, a surprise to me because he didn't mention it to anyone. He later confessed he didn't want Mom to know because she would get upset after what happened to our cousin and try to prevent him from going.

"Are you hurt?" I asked. "Did you fall?"

"Nah, I'm just sore," he said.

"How's that?" I asked, naively believing that skiing consisted of simply standing up and letting gravity do all the work.

"What?!? What do you mean? I have sore muscles because skiing is physically demanding!" he said as he got up and went to our room, mumbling. "Geez, this guy doesn't understand anything."

When I reached the 9th Grade, I went on Outremont High School's annual ski trip. I didn't at first consider going, but Johnny A. wanted to and convinced me to go with him, I guess because he preferred being accompanied by at least one friend. He brought me almost by the hand to the main office where the clipboard with the signup sheet was located.

I registered as Andreas "Hot Dog" Kessaris which was intended as an ironic joke because I knew I wouldn't be shredding the slopes. "Hot Dog" is a reference to an atrocious flick called *Hot Dog: The Movie* that was set at a ski resort; a juvenile, mid-eighties sex comedy starring Shannon Tweed that featured poor acting, awful ethnic stereotypes, tasteless humour, and lots of nudity. Johnny A. and Paps had dragged me there kicking and screaming. They loved the film. I was bored, and a few times offended, more so by its poor overall cinematic quality than its content.

I knew my mom would not let me go if I asked, but I had enough of my own money to pay the fee and I forged her signature on the permission slip.

During the bus ride up I asked one of the teachers, Mr. Kovalchuk, an avid skier, how long it would take.

"About an hour to an hour and a half, depending on traffic."

"That's pretty far," I said.

"Well," Mr. Kovalchuk said, "Mr. MacDonald lives up here and he has to drive this daily. He'll be waiting for us when we arrive. He's the one who organizes this whole thing."

Mr. MacDonald was one of the faculty at Outremont High. I didn't take any of his classes and still have no idea what he taught. He was a burly, sturdy man with glasses, a full, bushy mustache, and a sufferer of male pattern baldness. Years later I saw a news report when they captured the BTK killer and I thought: *Wow! He looks just like Mr. MacDonald!* One of his students, a chunky Yugoslavian kid, called him the "Bald Eagle" (obviously not to his face).

I showed up on the day of the trip in jeans, a sweater, a leather motorcycle jacket and matching gloves, and a tuque. My gloves were unlined and thin, providing little insulation from regular Montreal winters, not to mention the bitter, northern cold. By the time we arrived I had realized by observing the others on the bus that my attire was not going to cut it out there in the elements. They were well-prepared and properly dressed, and I was already starting to shiver, standing out like an ostrich in a chicken coop.

We lined up for our rental gear. Some of the older, more experienced kids helped me, Johnny A. and another rookie skier, a kid named Tasso P., put on our boots the right way and explained how the release catches on the skis worked, which for me was a waste of time because I didn't get a chance to remove them the proper way; I'd fall down and they'd pop off.

There was a small, man-made hill just outside the chalet's broad vista windows where we congregated. The instructor, a tall, slim living Ken doll with bright white teeth, wanted to see if we knew how to ski. He gave us a crash course ("crash" being the proper word in my case) on how to climb the aforementioned mini-slope by walking sideways, how to pivot the front of our skis inward to make what was called the "snow plow" to slow us down, and how to turn.

One by one we skied down while the instructor handed out passes to the proficient ones. In less than ten minutes all had earned their passes but me, Johnny A., and Tasso P. They were finally given theirs when they proved they could handle themselves on the hill, and then there was just me. Climbing up I kept sliding down backward and falling. When I made it to the top, I would employ the snow plow improperly and land flat on my face. The exasperated Ken doll, I think because he had somewhere to be, eventually gave me a pass and made me promise not to ski any of the difficult runs and exclusively use the beginner slopes. I agreed with the sincere intention of keeping my word.

I went to the T-bar and was partnered with Tasso P., a Ralph Macchio-type who wore nerdy checkered shirts and had a bad $5 haircut that was immature even for a ten-year-old, with a part on the right side. He, similarly to Macchio in his most famous role as the title character in *The Karate Kid*, was severely bullied. Tasso P. transferred out of OHS the next year. After graduation, I ran into him. He had changed his entire look, with a cool haircut and a slick leather jacket. He worked weekends at a parking lot and was able to purchase a sporty Mazda (considered a cool car at the time). Classic personal reinvention. I often imagined transferring to another high school and reinventing myself as well and becoming cool and popular, but now I know I would've failed and ended up right back where I was at the bottom of the social totem pole, in worse company.

The lift operator instructed us to stand, emphasizing that we were not to sit down, and let the T-bar pull us up. I did exactly that, but Tasso P. kept sitting down and falling off. The resulting slingshot effect threw me off as well and the operator had to stop the lift until we could get out of the way. He repeated the instructions to us, and Tasso P. immediately blamed me.

"It was that guy!" Tasso P. said, pointing his mitten at my face.

"What're you talking about?" I said. "You're the one who tried to sit!"

"No, *rhé*!" he said. "It was you!"

Tasso P. proceeded to fly into a rage and jumped around like a kangaroo on lava, reiterating that I was the one at fault. The lift operator told us to get back on because we here holding up the line. And again Tasso P. sat down, fell off the ride, and one more time I was thrown. Then it happened a third time, with Tasso P. continuing to insist I was the one responsible. By then those waiting for their ride up the mountain had grown impatient.

I asked the lift operator, "Can I go on the T-bar by myself?"

"Sure," he said.

So I got on the T-bar alone, and Tasso P. on the one behind me. A few seconds later we stopped yet again. I looked back to see Tasso P. flat on his face, looking up at me. I didn't say a thing. I knew I didn't have to; they found out who the real culprit was.

I disembarked at the beginner slope where Johnny A. had been skiing since he got his pass. He had a rough go at first but was now getting to the bottom smoothly and intact. I tried it and after a few attempts I made it down without falling. So I figured to hell with what the instructor said. I was ready to move up.

I took the T-bar all the way to the top and found what looked like a nice, simple path, completely missing the sign with the black diamonds, utterly ignorant of what it meant.

The first part was fairly easy. After a sharp turn, which I adroitly negotiated, I found myself at the top of what looked like, from my perspective, a vertical drop so high there were clouds between me and the bottom.

I halted my advance at the precipice and looked down the slope. At the foot of the hill was the chalet.

No way can I ski that, I thought. *I've totally fucked it up this time.*

I stood there for what felt like an eternity and a day, trying to decide what to do and if there was another way to descend the mountain without killing myself.

Were there any stairs anywhere? Is there a lift or T-bar I could take down? Perhaps someone has a parachute?

Then I felt an unexpected, sharp shove.

I went over the edge and started to descend. I quickly turned my head and saw a brief flash of Mr. MacDonald and a small group of popular kids cackling like hyenas.

That fucking bald asshole pushed me!

I immediately got into survival mode, focusing on the slope before me, trying to hold it together. I was gradually encompassed with panic as I accelerated, but fortunately, the path was smooth and had no moguls.

Around two-thirds of the way down, I surmised it was time to start slowing down for a smooth finish. With no time to waste I was ready to do … The Snow Plow!

Just short of the chalet I employed the technique. I don't know if I engaged it too quickly, improperly, or hit a rut in the snow but my legs were instantly pulled out from underneath me and I was catapulted face-first into the snow, sliding the rest of the way down on my belly in full view of the chalet. By then most of the kids from my school, including Johnny A., Tasso P. and this guy who ran with the popular clique that I first met years earlier in the Boy Scouts, named Peter P. (one of the more experienced skiers), were having their lunch.

I slowly slid to a stop and lay there motionless, my pride more injured than my body. My jeans, already damp from all my previous falls, had soaked up more moisture from the hill. It was not long before Mr. MacDonald and the other kids arrived at the bottom, now giggling like a bunch of anime schoolgirls, amused with their own antics.

"Not bad, kid. But you have to stay on your feet. Don't be a human toboggan," Mr. MacDonald said as he motioned to his little gang that it was time for lunch.

I wanted to get up and tell him to go fuck himself, then ram my ski pole so far up his ass that his shit would say "Rossignol" for a year. But like Mr. Berton, he was a teacher and I had no rights or recourse. Who'd take me seriously?

Angry and humiliated, I gathered up my gear and returned it to the rental shop. The attendant reminded me I still had time, but I ignored him, seething.

I went to the cafeteria and ordered a hot dog, fries, and a coke, took a seat alone, and ate them as I observed the long table where all the OHS kids had gathered, talking loudly about their runs down the hill. Peter P. had brought a grotesque werewolf Halloween mask and they had taken turns wearing it while skiing.

After lunch I bought a hot chocolate, sat at the window, and watched the others enjoying themselves as I did a slow burn. I was angry at the other students, angry at Mr. MacDonald, and angry because my Levis had soaked up an ocean of water and for sure wouldn't dry anytime soon. Johnny A. joined me and gestured towards a table where Mr. MacDonald was seated with other members of the OHS faculty.

"Do you think one day we'll be bald like Mr. MacDonald?" he asked.

"I don't know," I said.

"You going to ski again?" Johnny A. asked, after a short pause.

"No," I said, coldly, unsure if he meant today or again in my life. But it didn't matter; my answer was the same regardless.

"Well, I'm going back," he said, rising to leave. "By the way, [Peter P.] and those guys were watching you ski. They were making fun of you, especially because you signed on as 'Hot Dog' Kessaris."

Why wasn't I surprised that the subtleties of ironic and self-deprecating humour somehow eluded students from Outremont High School?

"Whatever," I said.

A few hours later we were loading into the bus for the ride home. I could not hide the intense shivering brought about by my drenched clothing. I was freezing. One of the Grade 11s came up to me and asked why I didn't wear ski pants. When I said I didn't have any he said I just should have worn a pair of sweatpants over my jeans.

"I don't own a pair of those either. But thank you, I'll remember that for next time," I said.

Johnny A. sat next to me on the bus. Peter P. and the others took seats in the middle section, obnoxiously laughing and whooping it up with stories of their adventures on the slopes, to the delight of all, while I sat at the back and silently stared out the window just wanting to be home.

"Andre," Johnny A. said to me, "those guys are jerks. They go skiing all the time. They laugh at you, but how good were they when they started? I bet none of them went on the difficult slopes their first time out. Look at me, I spent the whole day on the easy ones. I think you're really brave to try what you did. I just want you to know that."

"I wasn't brave," I said. "I was stupid."

When we arrived back at OHS, I knew most of the kids would walk down Bernard Street and take the 80 bus home, like I did daily. I had no desire to spend one more second with them.

The 119 Rockland bus ran along McEachran Street. It passed by twice an hour, and I would have taken it home regularly except for the fact that some genius at the Transit Commission scheduled it to pass five minutes before the school day ended, and then at 3:24 pm, making it impractical. If they had adjusted the time slightly I could have been home in twenty minutes instead of the thirty to forty minutes it otherwise took. Of course, the Outremont Metro station, which would have gotten me home even sooner, opened right on time: the September after I left OHS.

I knew the 119 was coming soon so I made a beeline for the stop the second we returned to campus and was soon on my way. My jeans were still soaked as I walked across TMR to the St. Roch gate into Park Ex, shivering from the merciless cold. By now the sun had set and the wind picked up as if it were planned just to inconvenience me; the gusts were like a thousand knives cutting up my legs, which were slowly growing stiff and sore.

I was soon home where I removed my wet attire, took a hot shower, slipped on a pair of pajamas, and crashed on the couch under a thick, warm blanket as I slowly nodded off, taking comfort in what Johnny A. had said.

COUPE DE VILLE

In 1980 my father's back finally gave out. He traced his problems to a tumble he took on an unseen patch of ice in the early 70s, made worse by the years of twelve-hour workdays he spent behind the wheel of his taxi. The spring and early summer found Dad lying on the living room floor in total pain, unable to work, so he rented out the cab he owned to another driver. Some evenings he would ask me, ten at the time but still rather pudgy, to walk barefoot on his back, which I did. He told me that it gave him some temporary relief.

Dad would have to go in for lower back surgery, with a lengthy recovery period. The day he left for the Lachine General Hospital he needed two men to help him to the car that would take him there. After six weeks away and a successful operation and rehab, he proudly ran up the stairs upon returning home, no longer in pain. The doctor told him not to work taxi anymore lest he reinjure himself.

So Dad found employment as a parking lot attendant. The company was owned by another Greek who hired mostly older Greek men. Dad worked at a small lot in Old Montreal Monday to Friday and another one downtown on Saturdays. He wasn't happy about it, but it provided for the family.

With his taxi rented out, we became a family without private transportation. We started looking for a new car for our daily use, spending summer afternoons visiting used lots around Montreal and answering ads in the paper, searching for a vehicle we liked at a price my father could live with.

Late one afternoon we were ready to give up and go home when my father spotted a place off of Jean-Talon Street West and Victoria. It was a Mercedes-Benz dealership.

"Mercedes?" my brother said. "Isn't that an expensive car?"

"Ahh," Dad said, "they may have a *uze-ed cah-ro* there that *eez* a trade-*een.* Sometime you find good deal there."

The dealership was half an hour from closing but they were helpful. I was outside with Peter and my mom as my father went in to talk to a salesman. I looked at them through the large dealership window, the salesman in his suit and Dad smiling and gesticulating.

He came out and declared: "He have a *cah-ro* he want to show us."

We went around back and waited at the service department as a thick, dust-covered garage door slowly creaked open, and out rolled a classy, grey 1977 Cadillac Coupe de Ville. The car had a hood so long it could be used as an aircraft carrier, and a trunk roomy enough to fit a couple of dead bodies, thus explaining its popularity with gangsters.

"What kind of car is that?" I said.

"*Eet eez* a Cadillac," my father said, "a fancy *cah-ro.*"

Mom was silent. Her eyes caught that car and it was love at first sight. This was the kind of ride her first employers in Canada owned. Now there was an opportunity to have the same kind of dream wheels.

* * *

My mother first left home at seventeen, two years after her father died, to go to Athens seeking steady work to help support her family. A few years later my grandmother recalled her to the small, remote mountain village called Rouvalis where Mom grew up. The Greek government, in horrible financial crisis, was looking to recruit young women, mostly from rural areas, to be trained and sent out to the English-speaking parts of the world as domestics. My grandmother saw this as an opportunity to better the family.

My mother was the chosen one. Her mission: to leave Greece, work abroad, and after attaining citizenship, be the bridge that would bring her siblings to a place where they could prosper. After years of war and political unrest, there was nothing for them in their homeland.

Why her? Mom was, unlike all of her siblings save for her baby brother, unmarried. She was fiercely independent and resourceful; the most cunning of the bunch. Not to mention she was hard-working, charismatic, and had movie-star looks. Who else but her to do this?

Mom signed up and was immediately sent to a boarding school where she was given a crash course in English. As she later described it: "They gave me a book that said A, B, C..."

She could have gone to the U.S., the U.K, or Australia, but ended up getting a placement in Canada. Mom went back to Rouvalis one last time to say goodbye to her family (she would not return again to Greece until 1977), and then took a boat that brought her to the port of Montreal.

Her new employers were a successful businessman and his wife with five children who lived in an affluent suburb in the West End of Montreal. The husband worked long hours and the wife was heavily involved in community and charity work; she would later go on to be a respected member of the Canadian Parliament.

They picked her up at the port and drove her to their home in his new Cadillac. They had small quarters for Mom in the basement with a closet, bed, radio, and her own bathroom. She was told to unpack her suitcase and get settled in. They took her out to dinner that night and then to a movie. (Mom claims it was *Guys and Dolls* with Marlon Brando, but this was 1960 and the film came out in 1955, although it might have been a repertory theatre.)

The next day the lady of the house discovered that there was nothing hanging in Mom's closet. When she inquired why she didn't unpack, my mom said she only had a blanket with her. (When Mom went home before leaving Greece and told my grandmother she was going to Canada, Grandma said that she heard it was cold there and gave her a warm blanket. It was the only thing in her small suitcase when Mom arrived in her new country. She literally came here with just the clothes on her back. She didn't even have a coat.)

Horrified by this, her new employer immediately took my grateful Mom to Woolworths and bought her a new wardrobe, a pair of decent, sensible shoes and snow boots for the winter.

When my mother's service contract was up after a few years, she decided not to renew and chose instead to strike out on her own to earn more money and be independent. When she attained her citizenship she began sponsoring her siblings until they were all here. All but one stayed in Canada permanently.

Mom often quarrels with her siblings, sometimes intensely; they regularly bicker and joust among themselves, switching alliances in the process.

She feels they are ungrateful, but to be fair they came here married, some with children, too distracted with their own struggles to stop and fully appreciate what she sacrificed for them at the behest of their mother.

***

Mom insisted that we buy the Coupe de Ville. Dad was a little apprehensive and being the committed Marxist/Leninist, he thought it was too bourgeois (he was a Chevy or Pontiac man; Oldsmobiles and Buicks were a bit too high-class for his taste), but I could tell a part of him was seduced by the idea of having a Cadillac. It was more than they wanted to spend but still affordable.

After a brief test drive, we went home and Mom and Dad discussed the car. A few days later they secured a bank loan and bought the monster, putting it in Mom's name instead of Dad's.

It became our family motorized vehicle for trips to the mall and vacations. Sitting in the backseat was like being on a comfortable couch. I felt like a V.I.P. Dad enjoyed driving the behemoth, although it was not something he would easily admit.

Around the time the car loan was paid off in 1983, my father came home on a Friday evening smiling from ear to ear.

"What's up?" I asked.

"I *djust queet* my *djob*!" he said.

"What are you going to do for work?"

"I take back my taxi Monday," he said.

"I thought the doctor said..."

"Ahh!" Dad said with a wave. "*Falk heem*!"

I was concerned for his back but happy that he would be returning to the taxi business. I could tell he hated the parking lot gig even though he didn't verbalize his displeasure.

What I didn't know was that my mother was to soon file for divorce. She had wanted to for some time but could not when Dad was laid-up with back problems. After that she wanted to make sure the Coupe de Ville was paid off; it was a plot to take the car for herself.

Diabolique.

It turned out my mother had originally got her driver's license in the 60s, surprisingly before Dad did, and used to own and operate her own set of wheels. She stopped after Dad took over the driving responsibilities, and now she wanted to regain her freedom. She asked me to show her how things like the lights and windshield wipers worked, and how to gas it up. Then she started driving the car herself. First around Park Ex, then to shopping malls, and when she was ready, directly to the divorce lawyer.

My brother was sixteen by then and had got his driver's license as well, so he had his time with the Caddy, taking it to high school on occasion, and a few years later to John Abbott College on the West Island.

Mom proudly enjoyed each moment with the Caddy, making sure it was constantly in pristine condition.

In my mid-teens, my mother took the Coupe de Ville out on a Saturday evening and did not return until 3 am. When I asked her the next day where she was she said she drove to the mountains. It turned out she took the Laurentian AutoRoute up north to St. Sauveur, where at night the lit-up ski hills could be seen from the highway. She stopped off in the small resort town and had a drink at a bar and hung out with a bunch of ski bums. (Apparently they failed to question what a middle-aged immigrant woman who didn't ski was doing there.) I later realized that for Mom, who was heavily sociable and decidedly not happy as a mere *hausfrau*, a night on the town was a luxury she seldom enjoyed while married. (In fact, numerous Greek immigrant women of her generation had insecure and old-fashioned, or "traditional" if you must, husbands who did their best to keep them at home and dependant, under a jealous eye.) Now there was no man in her life to tell her she couldn't.

That sort of behaviour was nothing new for my adventurous mother who was a rogue loner. She told me that when she was a teenager she would take the family mule Roussa out for evening rides, often going up to the mountain tops to gaze at the stars.

When my mom got divorced she was middle-aged but still had her looks. Almost immediately she drew the attention of our elderly landlord Mr. Davitz who wasted little time proposing marriage, promising to leave her the house when he died. (I did not find out about this until years later.) When I asked why she said no to him she said, "He was an old man and I *deed* not want *heem* to *taats* me!"

Mr. Davitz died a few years later. His daughter invited Mom to the funeral and insisted she be seated with the family at the synagogue service. She was even allowed to sit Shiva on the first night (all of which Mom considered a great honour), where Mr. Davitz's newly-divorced oldest son, a chartered accountant who made a good living, took his turn asking for Mom's hand in marriage, which she refused. She failed to explain to me the reason for that turndown.

I feared my time behind the wheel of the beast would not come, but when I came of age and got my license I had my own experiences with the Caddy. I remember the first time I put it in gear and lifted my foot from the brake. It slowly and smoothly moved forward; while large, it was forgiving and an ease to handle.

By 1989 the car was starting to become too costly to keep. Repair bills were getting larger and parts kept breaking or wearing out. The price of the gas it guzzled was perpetually increasing, and the insurance was more expensive. So Mom shopped around and found a buyer willing to pay top dollar for the classic road machine.

The last day Mom had the Coupe de Ville was a warm Sunday in late autumn. She took it out alone for one final all-day drive around the city. She went to one of her favourite parks on Gouin Boulevard and took pictures of the vehicle with her Polaroid Land camera. The next day she signed it over to the new owner for a hefty sum, not telling him she took the cigarette lighters as souvenirs.

For years she kept the pictures and lighters in a sort of makeshift mini altar. When she gazed at the memorial longingly and sighed it broke my heart. I found it odd that she would have such an attachment to an assembly of glass, steel, plastic, and rubber like she did; not being much of a car guy, it was a mystery to me. I mean, it was just a machine after all; it couldn't love her back. A person or even a pet that was gone I could understand, but a car? After she sold the Caddy she purchased a Buick that was newer and superior with her second husband (who was far from newer and superior). Why was she stuck on the Caddy? Did it remind her of good times? Was it the sentimentality? Or that she achieved her goal of having a dream car?

One day I finally asked her.

"It *reemind* me that *nah-ting* last forever," she said.

PERMANENT RECORD

I wasn't concerned with bad grades once my parents divorced. My father didn't live with us so he was easy to avoid and my mom didn't care much for none of that there fancy-pants book learnin'. I didn't want to become a doctor or a lawyer or an engineer. I had something else in mind. I spent more time playing guitar and listening to music than doing my homework. I would practice in my bedroom with the curtain up at night, looking at my reflection in the window and imagining myself shredding my axe in front of a sold-out arena crowd. I had no concern for what American high schools called one's "permanent record" because I knew I would eventually audition at Vanier's music program, be accepted based on my musical talent and proficiency, study for three years, and come out the other side ready to take on the music industry.

Today I know how unrealistic that dream was. Being a musician is not a trade like say, learning to be a mechanic or a carpenter, and Vanier College was not a trade school (I'm not implying that there's anything wrong with trade schools or that mechanics and carpenters are not skilled; it's just not the same thing), where one goes to classes, passes exams and gets an apprenticeship. It takes lifelong dedication and countless hours of practice to get to a serious professional level; music has to be your life. And you had to have a certain degree of natural talent, which I lacked. Just being a working musician is difficult enough. Making it big, even if a person had Paul McCartney's talent, is a million-to-one shot. When I was fifteen I had the emotional maturity of a ten-year-old. I thought I was cool and the general public just didn't realize it yet. I thought people liked me. I thought I could do it all.

When I took a summer course in theory and ear training at the McGill Conservatory of Music, I bought one of their T-shirts. It was nothing fancy; white cotton with a small red crest, but I liked wearing it around OHS when school started in the autumn. I had grown my hair into an ethnic afro and wore a leather motorcycle jacket in an attempt to ameliorate the rocker/guitarist/badass persona I was developing.

In Grade 10 OHS put on a career day for students in the gymnasium where recruiters from the police & fire departments and the army, as well as reps for fields like nursing, radiology, and other medical support professionals were looking for their next generation. People from trades like welding, carpentry, surveying and bricklaying were present too, but those vocations failed to catch my attention.

The school gave out forms asking what we were interested in to see if they could arrange visits to workplaces. I wrote "professional musician," much to the chagrin of Madame Zad, my homeroom teacher who, in front of the whole class, glared at me over her large old-lady glasses, the kind with the gold chain, and said: "*Tu ne devrais pas perdre ton temps avec des telles conneries.*"

Most of my friends got what they wanted. Big Jerry was interested in meteorology and got to go to the Dorval Weather Office for two days. Me? They didn't set me up in a recording studio. They didn't even ask for a second choice or send me to a record company or radio station, or maybe legendary Montreal rock impresario Donald K. Donald's office. (By the way, Donald Tarlton, the famous DKD, grew up in Park Ex.) They just blew me off like I was nothing.

"I want to be a plumber!"

"Sure!"

"I want to be a pharmacist!"

"Sure!"

"I want to be a fashion designer!"

"Sure!"

"I want to join a circus freak show!"

"Sure!"

"I want to be a professional musician!"

"Fuck you, Andreas!"

Big Jerry's assigned trip to the weather office was on a Thursday and Friday. When I saw him on the following Monday and asked how it went, he said, "Oh my God, Andreas, it was *soooo* boring! I couldn't imagine a duller place!"

They measure rainfall and temperatures and look at satellite images. What did he expect? That they would go out and chase down tornadoes and hurricanes?

"I tell you," he said. "The first day they sent me out to get them coffee and I felt like not coming back. I didn't even go on Friday! I don't want to be a meteorologist anymore."

(The weather office noticed his absence the next day and told on him to the school, who made Big Jerry write a combination thank you and apology letter for standing them up.)

A few days later during lunch period I was in the cafeteria with my friends and we were joined by a trio of girls who were not afraid to be seen with us. They were made up of Freddie, an Acadian, and her two best friends, one Hispanic, the other Ukrainian. The three of them were smart, well-dressed and pretty, but they were not Greek so for them ascending the social ladder would be difficult, although I think they were level-headed enough to realize the pointlessness of superficialities like high-school popularity.

Stretch, Paps, Johnny A., Big Jerry, and The Weasel were all relating their respective Career Day experiences, when I burst in without anyone asking me and started going off on one of my tangents about how the school snubbed my request. Then Freddie, with whom I hadn't had any problems in the past, said out of nowhere: "Y'know, Andreas, you grow your hair and wear a leather jacket and try and act like some kind of hot guitarist rebel tough-guy, but everyone knows you're not! You can hardly play guitar and you're the school wimp! Look at that T-shirt you're wearing! It looks like the kind they gave us for gym in elementary school. And everything that comes out of your mouth is shit!"

Our table was blanketed with an uncomfortable silence. She was loud enough to grab the attention of other students. I felt like I was hit in the face with icy-cold water; to this day I have no idea why someone who until that moment was pleasant, kind and friendly would explode at me like that. Was it something I said? Did I hit on a sore spot? I was so flabbergasted I didn't know how to respond; a witty rejoinder escaped me. The only think I could think of was to get up, try and gather what little remained of my dignity, and walk away. As I shuffled off, I could hear Stretch say to her, "Why did you do that? That was so mean," as Johnny A. expressed his disapproval with a "Not cool, Freddie."

Freddie was in my next class. She usually sat in the row next to mine, one seat back, and was already there when I arrived. I avoided eye contact and quietly took my seat. A few seconds later I was passed a note. It read: "I'm sorry about what I said."

I turned and looked at Freddie. She waved at me, looking a bit embarrassed, with an awkward grin and innocently batting her eyelashes. I motioned to her that it was okay. The rest of my time at OHS, she went out of her way to be extra nice to me. I didn't wear the McGill T-shirt again.

* * *

It was the mid-October of my final year at Outremont High School. I was in honours English and doing well enough that I was scheduled to graduate in the spring. During my time at OHS I had failed so many other courses that a majority of my classes were with grade 9s and 10s, and none of my core friends were in any of them with me. We would meet in the morning at our lockers, then say bye until recess, then bye again until lunch, then the final byes at the end of the day.

Those about to graduate were given forms to fill out for the yearbook. We were expected to detail our activities and what was abbreviated as "P.D." which meant "probable destination," i.e. where we thought we would go in life. At recess, I sat with Stretch, Johnny A., Paps, The Weasel, and Big Jerry and we all filled out our forms, which were due the next day. For P.D. I wrote "Centre stage at the Montreal Forum" and for Activities, I wrote "Rockin' Out!" ignorant of how silly that would look years later, even if my dreams did come true, especially next to my grad photo where I sported my failed Hendrix-like hair. The rest contained lyrics from a song I liked at the time and my favourite OHS memory, which was a school trip to Quebec City.

It was a nice, warm day outside. When lunchtime came, I wanted to walk to Van Horne Avenue where a restaurant sold pizza by the slice. A wedge and a Coke cost $5. The guys weren't interested, so I went alone. As usual, there was a line-up outside so it took a while to get my food and I ate it quickly on the way back to school. By the time I returned I felt something odd on the back of my head, like my hair was being tugged. I reached around with my hand to discover something sticky there.

What is that? I thought. I smelled my fingers. *Spearmint? What is this? No! Oh no!*

At some point in the day, probably between recess and lunch, some asshole had stuck their gum in my huge, thick hair.

I couldn't believe it.

Who had done this? Why? When?

I stood outside the school, not sure what to do.

I should've gone home. It was only two classes. I could've said I started to feel sick. But if I got caught I would get in trouble. Not that I minded trouble, nor would it be all that serious (my absence might not have even been noticed); I just didn't want to tell anyone this happened to me. I was so embarrassed. So ashamed. I dreaded the idea of people finding out, and then snickering and laughing at me behind my back.

High school is such a fucking prison. You need permission to do anything. A horrible place. That's why college and university were such a breath of fresh air. You can miss a class and nobody cares. You can get up and walk out in the middle of a class with impunity. In my first year of CEGEP, I did just that and skipped classes just for the hell of it because I could. Honestly, it felt good but I ended up failing a course my first year so I quit doing it by my second semester. My father was paying good money for my education this time around and I owed it to him to at least attend classes and make a serious effort.

I decided to push the gum a little further in so it would not be visible, and get through the day. My mother would not be home until after 4:30 and my brother, who at the time was a student at John Abbott College all the way out on the West Island, was rarely home, so I could get rid of the wad quickly.

It turned out to be the longest two hours of my life. In that time I went from fear and humiliation to anger and hate and back again. My anxiety level just kept going up and up like the elevator at the CN Tower, to the point where if anyone had spoken to me, even casually, I would have exploded, so I kept my head down and my mouth shut.

After the final bell, I went straight to my locker, gathered my things, and left as soon as I could. I wanted to beat the crowd to the bus and get home without having to deal with my schoolmates from Park Ex, some of them obnoxiously loud and boisterous. If they noticed the Wrigley's in my hair they would mock me ceaselessly and mercilessly. Rushing to catch the bus brought me back to Grade 7, where I made no friends so I had no reason to hang around the school. Peter told me on my first day not to carry around money because I'd be robbed. Sensing a weak animal in the herd, several bullies intended to turn the heat up on me, so I did what I could to get out before they could gather and organize, but instead all I did was make an even bigger spectacle of myself as I ran full speed to catch the early bus.

When I was in Grade 9 my midyear report card was such a catastrophe that my father took me to a friend of his who had a tutorial college located on Park Avenue and St. Viateur, right next to the YMCA. We went into his small office and Dad explained his dilemma.

Talking about me like I was not there, Dad said, in Greek, "He is an intelligent boy. Quite keen and sharp. If he comes back to your office here a week from now and you have one pen or something small out of place he would notice. He talks like someone much older; knows things a boy his age shouldn't know. He's like an encyclopedia. But he constantly gets lost in his own mind. I don't know what to do with him! And he is so lazy!"

His friend reassured him he could help me, asserting that he had a Ph.D. in education; in fact he mentioned his advanced degrees often. Although I didn't know it at the time, my father described to him a classic case of autism. Why didn't Mister, oh, sorry, *Doctor* Ph.D. know this? Once again an expert in education should have been aware and perhaps suggested some sort of alternative or specialized school with a different curriculum; one where I could have been nurtured, protected, and possibly prospered. Instead I was stuck in an under-funded dump with a horde of neurotypical half-wits who think it's a scream to stick gum in someone's hair. (Though to his credit, he did tutor me in math and French well enough to improve my grades and pass that year.)

I got off the 80 at Ball Avenue and sprinted home in case Mom or my brother would unexpectedly be there. My plan was to ice the gum, get it out, and shower. I only showered at night so if I did it the second I came home it would've aroused suspicion. I was relieved to find the flat empty. I tried the ice but it didn't work, or more accurately I was nervous, rushed, impatient, and fumbling the whole thing. I tore the place apart looking for the barber scissors, which eluded discovery, so I grabbed my mother's fabric scissors instead and in a panic awkwardly cut the gum out of my hair. I looked at it for a few seconds in my hand, wanting one more time to know who did this and wondering who was laughing at me right now. I quickly flushed it and took an intense shower. I cleaned up and was sitting on the couch watching TV when Mom came home.

I didn't practice guitar that night. I didn't do my homework. I just couldn't concentrate. The cycle of anger and hatred, for myself, then for others that had started in the afternoon kept getting worse.

Nobody likes me! I'm just a loser! I'm not going to be a rock star or anything cool! Fucking bastards!

Those thoughts kept circling around my head and I felt like I had no sympathetic ear to talk to about what happened.

The really frustrating thing about this incident is that I didn't have a specific target for my boiling rage; I had no idea who had done this to me or why. Was it someone who knew me and had a beef with me, or simply a random asshole? Why was I selected? Did they even know me? Were they male or female? One person or a group of people? What if it was a group of tough kids? I would be unwise to confront them lest I receive the beats of my life.

That night I went to my school bag and until this day I'm not sure what my reasoning was but I decided to change my yearbook form. I wanted to spew, so I erased my P.D. and put in "Terrorist and assassin" and for Activity, I put "Torturing small animals." I wanted to change some other things too but couldn't think of anything, so I would finish it another time. My goal was to have the yearbook editors censor what I wrote and it would appear in the book as either watered down or blank. Then I could complain that they were oppressing me and otherwise raise some useless and impudent stink, and the other kids would wonder what I wrote that was so inflammatory and *then* they would realize that I was a cool play-by-my-own-rules outlaw all along. That plan made perfect sense to me at the time. Today I don't understand how I ever thought it so; most students at OHS were clearly indifferent to me.

The next day was the deadline and although I had cooled down a bit, I decided to hand in the form as is. After a while I got over the whole gum incident. Then came spring, and yearbook day. I opened mine figuring they wouldn't allow something as tasteless and insensitive as what I had written in the yearbook. I was wrong. They printed it.

Because of my unpopularity, most people didn't notice, so even if I had written something awesome it would've been ignored. That was the good part. The bad part was when Mrs. Sheehy, one of my favorite teachers and an educator who got me and was my champion, read what I wrote and sought me out.

"Andreas, how can you write this?" she said, looking at me as though I had let her down. "You love animals. You talk about your cat all the time. Why did you do this?"

Up to that point in my life, it would've been difficult to make me feel real shame, but she did and I knew she was right.

High school for me was a waste of time. I can't say that enough. But I had some good friends. And a few good times. Quebec City was one. The Stratford trip was another. Wasn't all shit. Still glad to be away from there. Done with that. No, nothing about the 32% I got in math one year, or any other blotches in my file bothers me. I do not fear they will catch up with me. Hell, I doubt those records even exist anymore since the P.S.B.G.M. has long gone the way of the Great Auk.

And what is the one thing that remains? That stupid yearbook. The cherry on top of the turd sundae that was high school. And the worst part of all is that I did it to myself. My permanent record.

THE OFFICE

In the summer of my nineteenth year, I found myself out of work. I had secured employment as a courier, an easy gig to get. All I had to do was have a car, a licence, a pulse, and pass a simple ten-question test about where certain streets were. I got nine out of ten correct and wasn't totally insane, so they hired me on the spot and I started to work post-haste on straight 50% commission.

Despite my knowledge of the streets, I got off to a rocky start. They gave me no training, advice, or any words on how to do the job. They just cut me loose with a courier number and destination: a prestigious law firm in the Alexis Nihon complex. I did not know that they had delivery parking, so I double-parked on the street. It was a hot, humid Montreal summer day so I wore a fishnet tank-top and gym shorts, showing up to the front desk looking rather conspicuous. The receptionist was aghast and quickly informed me that pickups and deliveries were at the rear, and pointed me in the right direction, fumigating her desk when I left. At the pickup and delivery window I identified who I worked for and they handed me a whole bunch of small boxes and large envelopes. I quickly put my courier number on all of the waybills. Two minutes later another employee from my company came and said rather angrily that most were his. (My number on the slips meant I would get paid for those shipments.) The person who hired me failed to explain precisely how the whole system worked and that I was to ask for items specifically for me.

I had to call the dispatcher when I arrived for my next assignment. They had a courtesy phone that kept making a horrible noise when I dialed.

"Hey," I said to the woman at the window, "your phone's not working!"

"You have to dial nine first," the other courier said in a snarky tone as he scratched out my number on the various waybills and substituted his own.

I bumbled my way through a week of pickups and deliveries. I didn't receive any parking infractions, but more than once I locked my keys in my car. I wish I could say there was a moment where a wise veteran courier or a Yoda-like dispatcher took me under their wing and advised me to keep and extra set of keys on me or which places had delivery parking or to carry a notebook and pen or dress better. But that didn't happen.

When I factored in the cost of gas and the mileage on my late model Toyota Tercel I was simply not making enough for this endeavour to be a worthy enterprise, so after a week I quit. I needed a job for the off-season and most summer posts for students were filled.

I visited my father at the taxi stand and upon telling him my dilemma he suggested that I do what my brother Peter had done when he was in CEGEP, drive his cab. (He would take the car from noon until 4 pm on weekdays, and all day Sunday during the summer.) By then my father was almost sixty and looking to slow down a bit.

I was hesitant, primarily out of fear that I would be successful at this and it would end up being my career. There is, of course, nothing wrong with doing that for a living; it's honest work. For me this was not something that I felt I was meant to do. I wanted to be my own man and make it in my chosen field on my terms.

Dad explained that while the gig was not glamourous, at least I could do it and the job offered flexible hours so I could work as much or as little as I needed. And at the end of the day, I would have cash in hand. That perk really appealed to me.

I reluctantly agreed and asked him what the process was.

The first step was to get a class 4C (chauffeur's) license. It required me to pass a physical, so I got the necessary forms and went to my family doctor.

As I waited patiently for my turn to see him there was someone else in the waiting room, desperately clutching his lower right-hand side in obvious discomfort: A guy who had bullied me in elementary and high school.

I didn't know his name, but he had a bad reputation around Park Ex. I first encountered him at Barclay where he was a year ahead of me, but did not look it; he was in fact quite a bit smaller than me. I was walking home from school one winter when he ran up behind me and pulled the toque off of my head, and waved it in front of me. I got so angry I charged him; knocking him down and wrestling with him on the ground. What I did not know was that he had an accomplice behind me and was attempting to play "keep-away," a popular game with bullies. I was blind-sided by his partner in crime. They both tried to punch me but our thick winter parkas made it difficult, so they just ran off. A few days later he angrily confronted me in the school yard, demanding to know why I tackled him and didn't participate in the game of "keep-away" like a cooperative little loser.

"Well, why did you grab my hat? Why did you bother me?" I said. "What did I ever do to you?"

Surprised that I came back and suddenly realizing that I had size advantage and he did not have backup, he just said, "Fuck you!" and walked off.

When I arrived at Outremont High School he was already there. One day as I was leaving I ran into him. He grabbed me by my jacket, demanding a quarter. My father had taught me a self-defence technique he learned in the navy where if someone puts their hands on your lapels you point your arm down, making it as stiff as possible, and then spin it in a windmill fashion. I did so and it broke the hold The Bully had on me. I must have taken him by surprise because he paused as if unsure of what to do, or maybe he once again realized that I was bigger than him and he was alone, but I took that opportunity to walk away quickly. I did not want to engage any further, concerned he would be carrying a knife or some other weapon. My fears were justified a year or so later when I saw him in the back of the 80 bus headed to Park Ex. He was trying to impress a girl and pulled out a gun, bragging that he was able to convert a starter's pistol into a one-shot .22 calibre weapon that fired.

Now The Bully was whining and crying and begging to see a doctor. When told he would have to wait his turn, he went into the bathroom and collapsed. The staff at the office pulled him out of there and laid him out on a couch. I still got to see the Doctor before he did.

The Doctor didn't ask me any questions or examine me. Instead, he sat at his desk and filled out the forms while talking to his wife on the phone and immediately passed them back to me upon their completion.

"Aren't you going to take my pulse or something?" I asked.

"Why?" he said, covering the phone with his hand. "Do you have an artificial leg? Do you have a glass eye? Do you need a hearing aid? Have you ever been committed to a mental asylum?"

"No," I said.

"Well that's what they are asking," he said as he went back to his call and shooed me away.

The Bully was still lying on the couch moaning and writhing when I left. The next time I saw him was about ten years later on St. Roch Street. He was stumbling down the sidewalk in messy clothes and unusually long hair that covered most of his face, but I knew it was him. He was mumbling to himself and when he walked past a church he did the sign of the cross and voiced a barely comprehensible prayer.

Next step was to go to *La* Régie *de l'assurance automobile du Québec*, (or as informally referred to at the time, simply "*La* Régie." It has since become *La Société de l'assurance automobile de Québec* or *SAAQ* … not sure when or why it went from a "*Régie*" to a "*Société*" but okay, whatever), and take a driver's test. For that, I had to wait a couple of weeks. At that point, I already had my driver's license for years, but I guess they wanted to see if I had somehow become a worse driver.

Fifteen minute driving test: aced.

Then I had to take a thirty-question exam. I got twenty-nine of them correct.

The next step was to send in an application to the taxi bureau. They vetted me to make sure I had no criminal record and informed me that because of my ethnicity I had to pass a French test, despite the fact that I was born, raised, and completely educated in *La belle province*. According to provincial government regulations, one would have to have at minimum a Grade 6 level knowledge of French for that job. And passing that test meant I had the option of taking the taxi exam in English. (I don't know, with regards to government of Quebec standards, how good one's French should be to, say for example, work as an engineer or perhaps be a surgeon. I have total respect for the French language and understand the importance of speaking it well, and I have no issue with French being the only official language of Quebec; in fact, in my opinion, all Canadians should be proficient in both official languages. I believe that all schools between Newfoundland and B.C. should teach the two equally, and that bilingualism should be a requirement for all federal employees, including those in the military, RCMP, and Canada Post. And I believe the half-French, half-English "O Canada" should be the sole official one, and the only version sung anywhere. However, in all honesty, if I were about to have major surgery, how well the doctor conjugates an irregular verb is the last thing on my mind; if I were driving over a bridge, I do not care if the engineer who designed it knows the difference between *es*, *et* and *est*.)

Bureaucracy in my home province can at times be overwhelming in its scope. Years later I would be working at a record store that sold VHS movies and other videos. At the time such sales came under the jurisdiction of another "*Régie*," this time *La R*égie *du cinema.* (I don't know if it still does.) Each video was required by law to have a government sticker on it that contained the Quebec rating for age appropriateness. The aforementioned sticker made each unit cost $1 more than it would anywhere else in Canada. The $1 in question would go to funding *La R*égie *du cinéma* ... that was the scheme.

Government inspectors, usually late middle-aged women with short haircuts and glasses, would pass by the store on a semi-annual basis for inspection. They had badges and were completely unfriendly and humourless with the demeanôur of an F.B.I. agent on the trail of a serial killer.

The last time I had to deal with one of the *R*égie's finest, I was the manager of the store. She marched into the establishment and immediately flashed her I.D. I assured her of full cooperation from myself and my staff and told her if she needed anything we would gladly help, all with a friendly smile.

She was unimpressed and even a little angry and contemptuous as she began her inspection with a mild harrumph. After about an hour she came up to me and wouldn't so much as make eye contact as she filled out her forms and then handed them to me for signature.

"*Est-ce que tout est en bien ordre?*" I asked.

"*Cette fois, oui,*" she said.

So I guess I better watch myself next time.

The appointment for the French language test was easy to make. The agent over the phone was friendly and explained the whole process to me in English, no less. I would go in for a written exam, and if I passed I would have to take an oral exam with an agent.

When I arrived at the *OQLF*'s downtown office I was sent to what looked like a classroom. There were thirty or so student desks, each with a booklet, a multiple choice answer sheet, and a pencil, arranged in neat rows facing a large table at the head of the class, upon which was a bulky reel-to-reel tape machine. I was to locate the exam that had my name on it.

I sat waiting as the room slowly filled with people of a variety of ages and ethnicities. When it was time for the exam to begin a short, slim, casually dressed, bespectacled middle-aged man with long hair that was thinning on top and a pointy goatee entered the room. Without saying a word he sat at the large table and turned on the tape machine, which gave us our instructions.

The test was a series of fifty questions. The first question contained a picture of a pencil on the table. The recorded message would say:

Question numéro un:
Oú est le crayon?
Le crayon est:

- *A. Sur la table*
- *B. Derrière la table*
- *C. Sous la table*
- *D. Il n'y a pas de crayon*

The entire exam was essentially like that: insulting and patronizing. So much so that I wondered if it was deliberately designed to humiliate and ridicule those taking it. Because the test was completely written out on the page, one of the examinees went ahead of the recording, completing it in ten minutes and swiftly exiting the room to go for the second part of the process as soon as possible. I probably could have done the same, but erred on the side of caution and for once in my life took my time.

After the written test was over we were herded into a cavernous room lined with benches and chairs for our turn at the oral part of the examination.

There were four doors in the waiting room, each leading to a small office. I wondered if they contained two-way glass with some creepy inspector on the other side casually smoking a cigarette like something from a gritty police drama as they decided our fate as human beings.

The doors popped open and we were called in one at a time. When it was my turn my examiner was a woman in her early sixties who looked like a schoolteacher. She was friendly and asked me to have a seat and told me to relax. On her small desk was another reel-to-reel tape recorder (had the *OQLF* not heard of cassettes?) with a microphone that looked like it was taken from a radio station in the 1970s. I was expecting to see pro-French language propaganda posters on the wall á la North Korea but instead found the room plain and impersonal.

She turned on the recorder and informed me that I had passed the written portion of the test, although she didn't give me my grade and I did not have the presence of mind to ask. I was nervous and uncomfortable, but it wasn't anything she did.

The Examiner began by asking simple questions like how I was and why did I want to drive a cab. I became more at ease as we engaged in small talk.

After five minutes she unexpectedly turned off the recording device. I thought I had said or done something wrong, but she quickly said my French was fine and I had passed, stamping my application form and dismissing me, saying that my certificate of eligibility would be in the mail.

Next I had to make an appointment for the taxi exam.

My father drove me to the taxi bureau, which at the time was on the Metropolitan, and knowing I did not have a great track record with written tests, he gave me a pep talk. He told me to watch for a question about the *Théâtre de Quat'Sous*, a venue that in his words "only holds twelve *falking* people" but was on the exam when he took it in the 60s.

The taxi examination required a grade of 75% to pass, and despite having studied maps of Montreal I only managed a paltry 71% the first time.

When I told Dad that I failed the test he asked me if the question about *Théâtre de Quat'Sous* was still there. When I said yes he flew into a rage, exclaiming, "*Falking makalismeno quat'sous*! *Een* my entire life I no have to take *aneeeone* there, *salaba-beetch*!"

Rules of the taxi bureau stated that if one fails the test they can't retake it for three months. By then it was well into August so there went my summer job. I didn't go back to take the test again. Dad didn't bring it up, knowing that I wasn't really that interested. I kept the Class 4C on my license just in case I wanted to look for a job as a limousine driver or something. A few years ago the *SAAQ* contacted me and asked if I still wanted the 4C classification. If I did I would have to go through the whole process again and I didn't feel like it, so I said it was fine with me to go back to a regular license.

Over the years the taxi business has changed. Cars now carry grotesque advertisements on top (the money for which I heard does not go to the drivers, but rather the taxi association and owners). There are now decals on the side of vehicles indicating it is a Montreal taxi. And they accept credit cards. Some even have a large "*Bonjour*" painted on the side. Drivers use GPS to find their way.

Recently I was walking along Sherbrooke Street when a cabbie stopped me and asked if I knew where a particular address was. My father would have tied a rock around his own neck and tossed himself into the St. Lawrence River before he'd do that. Dad, like all the good drivers, knew the city backward, forward, inside out and upside down. It turns out I did know the address the driver wanted. Guess I missed my calling.

BARRY GREYSON

The University I attended in the early 90s was at that time not a place of great renown; for most it was a second or third choice. When *Maclean's* magazine rated Canadian universities and colleges, it perpetually ranked close to the bottom, if not dead last. (My alma mater at the time was less than twenty years old. Moreover, they have since worked hard and deservedly moved way up the rankings; moreover it is important to consider there were legitimate and understandable objections; for example, institutions which lacked MD programs were rated against schools like McGill or the University of Toronto.) However I remain proud to have gone there.

Two of my classes during my first semester were at a now-demolished building downtown. The place looked like an abandoned high school, with the feel of an institution where immigrants learn Canadian civics and history to pass their citizenship exams. My classes there were at night, and right across the alley, we could see aerobicizers working out at the adjacent "Y." A majority of the teachers were aging relics well past their "sell by" date who were hired when the university was incorporated in 1974 (although some of the best professors, and a number of my personal favourites, were among that group), or Ph.D. candidates at McGill who taught part-time and were hired last-minute to fill holes (who are as well ranked among my favourites).

Despite this the Communications Department enjoyed a reputation so grand that it attracted students from as far away as Australia, Norway, and South Africa, despite not having an internship program, like the equivalent department at the University of British Columbia, where a few of my CEGEP friends went. There they set you up with an unpaid radio, TV, or film *stage* for your last semester, easing you into a potential job. (One of my Dawson classmates who went to UBC ended up interning on a new science fiction production for the Fox Network. The show in question? *The X-Files*. They liked her so much she was hired upon graduation and she worked there as a production assistant throughout the show's time in B.C.)

I was beginning to think it was a mistake. CEGEP had gone well for me. It was the first time I not only enjoyed school but thrived; I had found a place that allowed me to be myself and my new friends really got me. Don't get me wrong, I had some great relationships with wonderful people at Outremont High, but I really connected with the gang at Dawson's Communications Department, and remain close to quite a few of them to this day. But the Communications Department at my university felt like a great leap backward; a return to the time of cliques and superficial popularity. In the end, it was the geeks and nerds, the techies who spent their time mastering editing, sound engineering, cinematography, and other difficult skills, who ended up working long-term in the entertainment business and travelling the world, while the cool ones—those who had ambitions to be the next Spielberg or Scorsese and were hip and popular—they all made meteoric disappearances after they went to Europe or Japan on their parents' dime to "find themselves"... Funny how none of them went to Borneo or Bolivia to do that, but I digress.

This was best exemplified by a class I took in advertising. It was loaded with the trendy, cool types with whom I had little in common. The Instructor was a stand-up comic who had worked in the ad game, but was not a Ph.D., or even close to that; for reasons unexplained she had a serious problem with actress Victoria Principal, referring to her as a "washed-up has-been" in the margins of one of my papers. (Long story as to why I would refer to Victoria Principal in my classwork.) She did know her craft and I have no serious complaints about the course itself; in fact, I received a respectable grade and learned quite a bit. But when The Instructor discovered that one of the students in the class was the daughter of a high-level ad executive in Toronto, she licked that girl's ass like it was a popsicle, and quite blatantly so. The others in the class? They had no problem with it, and some even did the same. When a group of us were outside on a cigarette break, I raised the issue. I objected to her showing such blatant favouritism, and for my efforts I was refuted and later totally snubbed.

The Instructor presented a slide show of various ads and we deconstructed them in class. One for cologne featured a black and white photograph of a fashionably dressed man with slicked back hair and a stubbly beard, in what looked like an argument with a flashy blonde woman in a party dress. The Instructor ridiculed the ad and made a joke speculating on the man's ethnicity, calling him a "Gino" and then grabbing her crotch and doing a stereotypical Italian man's voice. Most of the class laughed. I, and a few others, chose not to join in, objecting to the odd and completely unfair notion that people of Mediterranean heritage could be targets of ethnic slurs and that was considered acceptable, but if it were another group actions like those would be frowned upon.

When we had to break into groups for a final project, no one wanted me on their team. The Instructor spoke up on my behalf, going so far as to comment that my advertising journal (as an ongoing assignment we had to keep a journal of our experiences and opinions on advertising and publicity we came across in daily life; thus the aforementioned Victoria Principal incident, which I guess is not *that* long a story after all), was one of the better ones in the class. But there were no takers.

"It's okay," I said. "They wouldn't let Rudolf join in any reindeer games either."

While that comment elicited a smattering of laughter, there were still no takers.

Finally, someone put up her hand and took me into their group.

I hated group assignments because it rarely became the true collaborative effort and team-building exercise it was intended to be, but rather a battle of egos. Often a dominant force takes things over and doles out assignments, and there is usually some lazy bozo who does not contribute at all. In this case, two guys in my group, both from England, took over the team and more or less imposed their will on us. My ideas, which were no worse than anyone else's, were summarily dismissed and each time I spoke I was ignored or talked over. So it was my turn to be the "lazy bozo." When we had a meeting in the small apartment of one of the Limeys (as I started calling them) on Park Avenue between Van Horne and Bernard, I just sat on the couch and watched *Jeopardy!* with the #1 Limey's girlfriend. My main contribution to the group: I was the only one with a car, and I drove #1 Limey to campus with his bulky early 90s Mac computer, which was an important part of our presentation. While I can remember the faces of all on our team, I can't recall their names. And I rarely spoke to any of them again, save for #1 Limey, who a few years later came into the record store where I worked, unpleasantly surprised to see me there. He was still with the same girlfriend but had left the media industry to become a carpenter or organic farmer or something like that, I don't know, I didn't really pay attention to him when he spoke. While I'm sure he's happier in whatever he's doing now, he was a totally arrogant asshole so I don't care; like a sizable portion of the people in that class, he had all the depth of a wading pool.

Fortunately for me, I had a Minor in English Literature that kept me grounded. I started off in the English Department and found the less "happening" and decidedly less shallow students there more to my liking.

In my middle year, I took a course in American Literature that would change the direction of my life. I still recall the first day of class on a sunny, warm September afternoon at the University's West End campus. We were a motley assortment: some English Majors, mostly artsy-nerd types (including a professional musician and actor), a few mature students, two women in their 30s (one a single mom), a retired woman who was there for I'm not sure what reason, an Italian guy who looked like Bruce Willis, and a scattering of others. We were primarily in our 20s but there was one teenager: a short, red-haired girl named Ginger.

Our teacher did not so much walk into class as make an entrance, his appearance conveying more statements than I could count on one hand. In his early 30s, he was tall and muscular, clad in large motorcycle boots, tight black jeans, a frilly, laced V-necked white pirate shirt, and a well-worn leather biker jacket. His curly blonde hair was receding and his beard was short and well-coiffed, covering a steam-shovel jaw. His teeth were spaced rather far apart; enough that he could probably floss them with a rope. Slung over his shoulder was a book bag so old it was losing molecular cohesion. On the shoulder strap was a large button that read "Kill McGill." A person whose charisma could take up a whole room, and linger long after he left.

He introduced himself as Barry Greyson from British Columbia, and said he was a doctoral student at McGill. (I was at first unsure why, if he were pursuing a graduate degree at McGill, he would want to "Kill McGill" as it were, but I later discovered that he was once a University of Toronto student and the button on his bag had something to do with a football rivalry.) His shrilly voice was firm and confident. He began by passing out the syllabus and explaining what we would be learning in the course and what books to buy. Then he went around the room and asked our favourite books. When he got to me I said, "*The Catcher in the Rye*."

"You read it in high school?" he asked.

"Yeah," I said.

"And did you think you were Holden Caulfield?"

"Yes, I did!" I said.

"Who here thought *they* were Holden Caulfield when they read the book?" he asked the class. Most of them raised their hands. Then he moved on to the next student.

Why did he do that? What was he trying to prove? Should I be insulted? Is this a joke on me?

The class met twice weekly, and as a group, we started to bond. I quickly made friends with a guy named Mike, an aspiring writer a few years older than me that I nicknamed "Iron Mike," (after a now-deceased professional wrestler named "Iron" Mike Sharpe who billed himself as "Canada's Greatest Athlete"), and a guy named Rick whose brother was a classmate of mine in the Communications Department. In mid-October Barry invited us all to his place for a party.

I was working as a service station attendant on weekends so I had to miss a shift to attend. I really wanted to go. Most of the class showed up at his flat on Clark Street and Mont-Royal Avenue. I was the first person to arrive. (Uncool as I was and still am, I didn't know that it is considered gauche to show up at the party's exact start time.)

Barry was there with his girlfriend. She was classy and suave, intelligent and sophisticated, with long, shiny, thick, curly black hair. I later discovered she was from New York City and her father made a fortune on Wall Street. Quite a contrast from Barry, whose father out west worked in the lumber industry, and not as an executive.

The evening went well, only marred by my getting drunk and making a clumsy and unsuccessful pass at one of the mature students from the class (the one in her 30s who was not a single mom).

By November the class had grown so close that we, including Barry, would hang out after our Thursday afternoon sessions. Sometimes we would go to a café, other times we would go out for drinks or to an NDG bar to shoot pool. I started to learn a lot about him; for example he was a recovering alcoholic, he made a living as a professional card player for a while, and had moved to Montreal about three years earlier.

After the Christmas holiday, Barry was kind of deflated. It turned out he had broken up with his girlfriend, and so we started spending even more time together as a group.

One day after the Tuesday class, Barry approached me, uncharacteristically anxious, and asked if I was doing anything. I told him I was going home.

"No," he said, "you're coming with me."

"Where?"

"Cyndie and Lyndie invited me to their place and you're coming with me," he said.

Cyndie and Lyndie were two students from the class. They sat together and over the course of the semester I learned that they were best friends since kindergarten, having both grown up in the same upper-middle class Montreal suburb. Cyndie was fair-skinned, thin, with blonde hair and blue eyes. Lyndie had a darker complexion, and was shorter and curvy, with curly brown hair and exotic eyes to match. They were both artsy, but Lyndie was a little more committed—she had tattoos on her upper arms, one of a skull with a top hat on, the other a serpent wrapped around a sword, having got them way before they became so commonplace; so yes, she was in it for the long haul. Cyndie, on the other hand, would soon enough abandon her artiness after university and opt to marry well and become one of those housewives that could be found at the Metro grocery store on Sherbrooke Street in Westmount on a Tuesday afternoon clad in yoga pants, white ankle socks, and a loose sweatshirt, killing time between coffees with the other soccer moms and picking up her kids at school in her massively oversized SUV; the kind of woman who at middle age would have multiple cosmetic surgeries and Botox injections to keep a young appearance in a futile attempt to prevent her orthodontist husband from banging his new twenty-year-old receptionist.

"I don't want to go," I said. "I'm going home. I have assignments to do."

Barry tensed up. The former high school football player expanded his broad, muscular frame and took a step closer to me so that he was right in my face. "You're coming with me!" he said.

"Why do you want me to go?" I said. He explained that he was going to try for Cyndie and needed a wingman.

Was he allowed to do that? I thought. *I'm not sure any of this is kosher!*

I went under protest.

Cyndie and Lyndie lived in a basement apartment in NDG, less than a five-minute walk from the campus. The three of them sat on the floor, Cyndie and Lyndie at one end of the living room carpet, Barry coolly lying with his legs splayed on the other end, propping himself up on his elbows and acting so nonchalant, as if they should be in awe of his mere presence; a far cry from the tense goofball who cajoled me into going there. He kept his sunglasses on the whole time.

After realizing that they were indifferent to my presence and no one there had any interest in me or anything I had to say, I stretched out on the couch and listened to their conversation, my head going back and forth like I was watching a tennis match.

After about an hour they declared they had another class to go to and so we left.

"Well, that was a waste of time," Barry said. "Where are you going now?"

"Home."

"Do you have your car?

"Yeah."

"Good, give me a ride home."

"It's a bit out of my way ... but ... okay."

The semester ended soon enough, and we had another party at Barry's place in May. When I showed up I saw something that took years off my life: Barry and Ginger were holding hands and being all lovey-dovey. He had not mentioned to me he was so much as slightly interested in her, but there they were, she acting as his co-host and bragging about their relationship. Once again I asked myself if this was allowed, but she was over eighteen and the class was finished, so I told myself this was not my concern.

Later that summer Barry called and asked if I wanted to meet him at a coffee shop. I did and was surprised to discover it was just the two of us. He was a little down and lamenting that his relationship with Ginger didn't work out, and the single mom from our class was calling him up, saying that he had "a moral obligation to sleep with her." When I asked he said that he didn't and wasn't about to, adding that she was a "crazy bitch" and that he told her if she called him again he was going to the police. On top of all that, the retiree in the class threatened to sue him for failing her.

"What's her problem? She didn't hand in one piece of work!" he said.

The following semester Barry had another party and invited me. I thought there would be people in attendance from last year's class, but I was the only one. (I don't know if I was the only one invited or the only one who showed.) It was there that I met Sylvie, who would be my girlfriend during my last year at university.

Barry and I would hang out at the campus coffee shop on occasion during that year, but we otherwise didn't see much of each other. My relationship with Sylvie died around graduation time and it really hit me hard. So much so that I lost touch with Barry out of fear that I would run into her at one of his parties.

A few years later I was working at a record store, unable to find any steady work in my field. I was trying my hand at writing, but not getting anywhere. I had strayed from the artsy/indie community and was looking for a pathway back. Then one day while reading *The Mirror* I came across a picture of Barry. I did some research and discovered that he had left academics and was now putting on underground shows and managing bands. Through a mutual acquaintance, I was able to get his phone number and left him a message. He did not call back. Answering machines were a little unreliable at the time so I left another message. Again there was no reply. Then a fortnight later he called me and left a message on my machine, saying, with what I felt was a hint of desperation, that he wasn't trying to duck me, and wanted to hang out again. After a long game of telephone tag we were able to connect and he invited me to a show he was putting together at a bar on Mont-Royal and de Bullion Streets.

I enjoyed the show but running it occupied his time and we didn't have a chance to catch up, so he invited me to another one he was doing a week later. He told me to arrive early this time so we could hang out. When I got there he was talking to the singer from the B.C. musical duo he had booked. She was a melancholy brunette in a tight, low-cut red and white striped top and mini-skirt, who wouldn't so much as look in my direction and dismissed me outright after being introduced.

"Andreas was one of my students a few years ago. He used to quote Rush in his term papers," Barry said to her.

"Guys who like Rush are sexist assholes, like the guys who dig Led Zeppelin," she said.

For the record, I only quoted Rush once during a class discussion about choices, where I said: "If you choose not to decide, you still have made a choice," a line from the song "Freewill."

I watched her perform and the act was haunting; almost mesmerizing … like nothing I had heard before. Afterward, I went up to the singer to tell her that I enjoyed the show.

"See," she said. "I'm not a total bitch."

"I didn't say you were a …"

"Here," she said, handing me a folded piece of paper, "have a poster."

"Uh, thanks," I said, accepting the poster and leaving.

When I got to my car I unfolded the paper to see a large cartoon of a ginormous vagina, presumably hers.

"It figures," I said out loud, laughing.

As time went on Barry would invite me to his shows, both large and small. He would host those galas, and once when he was performing he asked me to introduce him. I didn't know what to say, so I got up on stage and improvised: "When D.H. Lawrence sent his publisher the manuscript for *Lady Chatterley's Lover*, the publisher replied 'for God's sake do not publish this book!' Guess he didn't know anything. And speaking of not knowing anything, ladies and gentlemen, here is Barry Greyson!" Then Barry took the stage and did one of his famous rants, and the audience ate it up like grandma's peach cobbler.

The crowd liked the intro. I thought Barry would be pissed, but he told me he thought what I said was cool, and from time to time he'd ask me to do the same thing at other shows.

One night after a show at the Casa del Popolo, the indie cafe on St. Laurent Street where a number of these events took place, two attractive, university-age French-speaking attendees hung around and started to talk to us. Correction, they talked to *him*. And flirted and fawned over *him*. I was completely ignored. After a while, Barry wanted to go home and asked me if he could get a ride, despite the fact that he lived three blocks away. Then he said I should drive the young ladies back to their flat, insisting I take him to his place first. Barry sat in the front with me as the girls gushed and swooned, and after I left him off I asked where they lived. They stayed in the backseat like I was their chauffeur and didn't give me an address, just a general direction and a vague intersection. The whole time during the ride they ignored me and just talked to each other, saying things like: "Barry, *il est magnifique*!" with the other one agreeing "*Oui, oui*!"

When we arrived at the corner they wanted, I stopped the car and asked, "*Est-ce que c'est ici*?" but before I could finish my sentence they got out without so much as a "*merci*" and walked away, not even bothering to close the car door.

The next day Barry called and asked if I had scored with one of them.

"Scored!?!" I said. "What the hell are you talking about? They wanted nothing to do with me!"

"So you didn't even try?" he said. "After all I did to set you up?"

"Try? Set up? Wha …"

"Yeah! Why didn't you at least try?"

Why is he even asking that? He was there. Didn't he pay attention? He didn't "set up" a damn thing. Those girls had no interest in me at all! What is wrong with him?

A little while later Barry asked me over to his place. He and some of his friends were going to get together and do something. When I arrived he had just gotten out of the shower and was wrapped in a long, white bath towel like he was Socrates, and lazing in his recliner, having recently shaved his head. He kept going on about how he didn't want to go out, and that the two of us should just hang out there and watch *Saturday Night Live*.

It was not long before the first of his friends, a folk musician I had seen perform at one of Barry's galas, arrived. He was shy and didn't say much, but it felt like he was surprised I was there, giving me a dirty look upon arriving. A few others showed up, saying that there was a big band dance at the Portuguese community center on St. Urbain.

During that time in the 90s, big band music had a strong but mercifully short-lived comeback. When we got there we found an enthusiastic group of people dancing to recorded music. Some were dressed like it was World War II, a guy even clad in an old-time sailor suit. One couple in particular tore up the floor.

My whole life I tried to avoid dancing. I am incredibly uncoordinated and oversized, and fear accidentally injuring not only my partner but others on the dance floor. Barry and his entourage, intimidated by how good some of the dancers were, became wallflowers, watching the spectacle with angry contempt. I stood with them and when a pretty blonde came by I asked her to dance. Barry's gang laughed at me, but she agreed. I thought I would at best get a polite "no, thank you."

"Were you in the class?" she asked.

As it turned out, the people there were taking lessons in the jitterbug, or the Charleston, or whatever the hell that dance was called, and this was the party where they got to strut their stuff and show off what they had learned.

"No," I said looking at the floor, "sorry."

"That's fine," she said. "I'll show you."

She took my hand and led me out on the floor. She gave me careful instruction, and I must say I did quite well and enjoyed myself. When I looked back at the group, they were amused, except for Barry. After a few minutes, the blonde said she wanted to join her friends and thanked me for the dance. I then thanked her and went back to the group.

"We're leaving this place. This is lame," Barry said.

"Okay, give me a minute I want to get her phone num ..."

"She doesn't want your number. Look!" he said, pointing to the blonde. She was holding hands with one of the guys in her gang. "Let's go!"

So we left and went for drinks on The Main.

Not long after that Barry asked me over to his place to hang out again. He invited a guy he knew named Fergie as well. It was the first time I had met him. Fergie was short, thin and had a fish face; in fact, he looked like a largemouth bass with glasses. He brought two women with him: one was a Francophone in her late twenties with spiked punk-rock hair dyed an unnaturally bright orange and dressed in raggy, alternative attire. The other was a shy, beautiful, well-dressed Japanese student who was probably twenty or twenty-one. The whole night they sat on either side of Fergie, who dominated the conversation. The Punker hardly said a thing all night, and was clearly annoyed the entire time. The Japanese student, whom I will call Asuka, smiled politely and did not seem at first particularly fluent in English. Fergie spoke to her slowly and used condescending, exaggerated hand gestures.

At one point I spoke directly with Asuka, who understood me with little to no problem. We discussed an incident in the news a year or so before where an American man shot and killed a Japanese student who was on his way to a costume party because he didn't know the term "freeze!" Asuka said that after that, before they travel to the U.S., students from her homeland are taught the meaning of "freeze" and similar idioms used there. Our conversation irked Fergie, who wasted no time intervening and steering it back to where he wanted.

We shared a joint (Asuka and Barry declined) and eventually the trio was off. I stayed behind and we watched *Saturday Night Live*. During the lame musical guest, Barry explained to me their unusual, almost disturbing dynamic.

"You see the Punker there, she is sleeping with Fergie and thinks she's his girlfriend, but he doesn't see it that way. He wants a piece of that Japanese chick. I don't think he has got it yet, but you see how much he wants her, eh?"

"How did he meet her?" I asked.

"She's a foreign student. Fergie teaches ESL. She's in his class."

"You mean she is currently one of his students?"

"I think so. He told me they met a few weeks ago," Barry said. "And the Punker? She was also at one point one of his students."

So this guy is using his job to build a harem. Talk about fringe benefits.

As time went on I started dating a nurse named Lana and saw Barry less often. When I did it was without her, and Barry started acting peculiar, even for him. He would keep asking to borrow $5.

Then I made the grievous error of bringing Lana to one of his shows. When I introduced them beforehand he was uninterested in meeting her and borderline rude. After the show (which Lana hated) he asked me for another $5, which I lent him.

On the ride home the consistently suspicious and perceptive Lana asked if I lent him money often.

"He owes me about $20."

"Oh! My! God! You are such an idiot! I can't believe how stupid you are," she said. "You know he'll never pay you back, a guy like him! Why do you do that?"

"He's my friend," I said.

"Well, I have friends and they don't ask me for money."

From then on, each time I went to any of his shows she told me two things: "Don't loan him anymore and get your money back!"

I ignored her orders. Barry was constantly broke; I couldn't say no.

Over time this continued, and Barry became progressively more depressed. Another girlfriend left him, and he would often call me in the middle of the night, describing to me episodes that sounded like anxiety attacks.

Meanwhile, I was having my own problems. My relationship with Lana was on the rocks after two years. By the time it was over I was working in the banking business.

A few weeks later Barry asked me to see a band play at the Casa. Afterwards we all went to the lead singer's place and passed around a joint. I was driving, so I didn't have any. Neither did Barry. The Singer droned on about how he didn't have a deal with a record company because they would fiddle with his music and ruin his artistic vision. Probably didn't occur to him that the reason his band remained unsigned was that there was nothing exceptional about them artistically or conceptually, and add to that they were not particularly good musically.

"Well, that is their right," I said. "They are, after all, taking the financial risk."

Dead silence in the room. After a beat they all started conversing as if I had said nothing. Then one of his bandmates broke out a candle and needles and I was quick to excuse myself. Barry left with me. Maybe they would get a recording contract if they worked harder on their music and took less junk?

As we walked to my car Barry said, "You make such a good first impression, don't you?"

I had just bought a Plymouth Laser off of The Weasel, a car that ultimately turned out to be a pricey lemon. Barry was impressed with my new wheels.

"You must be doing well at the bank," he said.

A while later we'd be hanging out at a certain place, and Barry would step away from me to go with two or three others down to the basement for almost twenty minutes and purposely not invite me to come along. When I finally asked him what was downstairs, he said it was just a small lounge for regulars to hang out.

But then why was *I* not invited?

When it came to being excluded from cool activities, he didn't know with whom he was dealing; I was no fool. I knew what they were doing down there, which began to concern me. Did Barry fall off the wagon?

Meanwhile the breakup with Lana continued to hit me hard, so I decided to go to Niagara Falls on Labour Day weekend in an attempt to relax, enjoy myself and get her out of my mind. On my way there my cellphone rang. It was Barry. I had not seen him for a few weeks. He urgently wanted to talk to me.

"Barry, I'm not in the mood right now. I'm hurting over Lana and I need to get away," I said.

"Where are you?"

"I'm on my way to Niagara Falls."

"Oh, you should have called me! We could have gone together," he said.

I was shocked.

Why would he say that? He didn't have the money to go there! Did he think I was going to pay for him? And he wasn't the type of guy to like Niagara Falls anyway.

"I'll call you when I get back," I said.

Monday afternoon I was on my way home, feeling better. My cell rang again. It was Barry, still desperate to see me. I asked what was going on, but he wanted to tell me in person. When I persisted, he admitted that he was broke and wanted me to pay his rent.

I had had enough. I blew my stack and told him off, hanging up the phone in disgust. I was working a job I didn't like and my relationship with the extravagant Lana, which had included a pricey trip to the Dominican Republic, as well as my new ride, had put me way in debt. I had spent what last few dollars I had on the trip to Ontario and now he wanted me to pay his rent. I just couldn't handle it. I had my own problems to deal with.

I didn't call Barry back or try to contact him again after that day.

Years later I was working at a credit card call center and became friends with one of the other employees, a guy from Ottawa named Marty who spent most of his time in the underground community, often attending shows at the Casa.

One day after a shift a few of us were eating at a Chinese restaurant when I dropped Barry's name.

"You know Barry Greyson?" Marty asked.

"Knew him," I said, and I related to him the story of the last conversation I had with Barry.

"Barry's a cool guy," Marty said. "Once I almost got into a fight with a guy at the Casa del Popolo, and Barry broke it up. Played peacemaker. I love his shows and rants. He's awesome."

"How is he?" I asked. "When was the last time you saw him?"

"He moved back to B.C. right after he did his last show here. The one where he came out of the closet."

"What!?!"

"Yeah, he did this great show where he went on about all his problems with mental illness and anxiety … it was rather moving … and the last thing he did was confess he was gay."

"Are you serious?"

"Yeah," Marty said. "You didn't hear about this? It was a big deal."

Gay? But he had all these girlfriends. He was hitting on women all the time. He had women crawling all over him. What the hell?

I often wondered why Barry kept me around if I didn't fit in with his friends. It didn't even occur to me that this could have been the reason.

But was it? Just what *was* all that about? What was his deal, really?

* * *

Twenty years later I found myself headed for home on the 80 after working a book fair. I was riding with someone I remembered vaguely from those days. We struck up a conversation and I mentioned Barry.

"Yeah," he said, "he was an odd character."

"Was?"

"Yeah, he died a few months ago. You didn't hear? Leukemia."

"What?" I said. "He died?"

"I'm sorry. I though you knew."

"Wow. Leukemia," I said. "He did smoke. And drank diet soda by the gallon."

"He did other things as well," he said. "He never really got his act together."

"That's a shocker. I had some unresolved issues with him. The last time we spoke it didn't go well."

"Yeah. Me too. He was like that with a number of people. That was him: a bit of a Svengali."

"Did you see or hear about the show when he came out of the closet?" I asked.

"No, I didn't. But Barry? Gay? I don't think so. He dated a lot of women, including one of my ex-girlfriends. Knowing him it was probably just shtick," he said, as he exited the bus.

Shtick? I thought to myself. *Really*? *Shtick*?

I guess Barry's whole life was shtick.

THE INTERNSHIP

My life after university was not what I had envisioned. I thought all I had to do was apply to TV or radio stations, or perhaps some production company, and in time they would call me for a low-level position. If I were to impress them I might move up over time, like in any other profession. Instead, all I heard was silence. My queries went unanswered. I got nowhere. My first post-graduation payroll job was at a mall record store. Although fairly knowledgeable about music, it was my expertise in movies that got me the gig.

A few years in we hired a part-time worker who was going to the same communications program from which I had graduated. His status made him subordinate to me, the full-time employee. At the end of the day one of the part-timer's duties was to vacuum the store, with a small red and black vacuum cleaner named "Henry." When I told him to do so he became upset and felt he was too good to do what he regarded as manual labour, questioning my authority and forcing me to take up the matter with the manager.

The part-timer's father was a local member of the National Assembly and when he ran for re-election he opened his campaign office in the mall, just a few stores down from us. When some bigwigs from a local radio station went there to interview him, he mentioned that his son wanted to be in broadcasting. They hired the son on the spot and he quit the record store and dropped out of school to work at the station. (He did have extensive on-air experience in college radio and as a live D.J., so it wasn't like he couldn't do the job.) At the time I became bitter, the sort of person my cousin Noula would describe as a "jealous pickle," at what I felt was unfair (even though I had no longing to be an on-air personality, I wanted to write copy or work in a production department), and didn't congratulate him when I found out. In fact, I was outright childish and rude. It wasn't his fault I couldn't find my way past the gatekeepers. And what would I have done in his place? Would I have said no? After I had a chance to cool down and grow up a bit I sought him out and offered an apology, which he was gracious enough to accept. If that outburst taught me anything it was that I had a way to go in the maturity department and I was ill-prepared for that kind of occupation. A few days later he walked by the store as I was vacuuming up with Henry. He knocked on the glass to get my attention. When I looked up, he pointed at me and laughed.

His replacement was Hill, who was about to start studying communications at my old university (popular program, eh?). She would go on to become one of my best friends of that era.

A year into her tenure at the store Hill asked the manager not to book her on Saturdays anymore. She had secured an unpaid internship with a production company. When I asked how she found out about it she said they posted ads on the Communications Department online bulletin board. I didn't have internet at that time and was so far behind the technological curve that I had no idea one could seek such professional opportunities in cyberspace.

She was beaming when we met for a coffee after her first day as an intern. She told me they taped several shows on alternate Saturdays that consisted of interviews, debates, and discussion groups featuring renowned authors, journalists, scholars and politicians, for broadcast on the CBC News Network and the Vermont and Upstate New York PBS stations. Hill was so excited she tripped over her own words as she imparted to me her experiences and while I smiled on the outside, inside I was once again a bitter, envious jerk.

About a month later Hill quit the record store. The production company offered her a paid part-time position and she didn't have enough time for school and two jobs. I was happy for her, but it was getting to me.

Why can't I find an opportunity like that? I kept thinking. *What am I doing wrong?*

One night we were at our favourite coffee shop on Hutchison and Fairmount and her enthusiasm was even greater than the last time. Then I asked if she could help me get a job there. Her illuminated face quickly turned dark and sour.

"Y'know, Andreas," she said, as she braced to deliver unto me a scolding, "you so totally always ask for people to do things for you but you, like, don't ever do things for yourself. You just sit around and expect people to hand you things just because you, like, want them!"

"That's not true," I said. "I have tried to find work in the industry …"

"Really?" she said. "Really? Do you think just going around and handing out CVs is going to, like, do the trick? Omigod it so totally is not!"

I was a little jarred. I had not seen that side of Hill before. It was like her whole bright, sunny personality had flipped into someone I did not recognize. I was a tad offended, but it was what I needed to hear. I couldn't find a single argument to defend myself. How could I? All her observations were, admittedly, accurate.

Noticing how what she said had hurt me, Hill settled herself and wrote a phone number on a piece of paper.

"Here," she said. "Call the production company and ask if they have any room for a new intern."

I thanked her and did as she said the following Monday. The woman at the production company told me to come in at a certain time and talk to the Executive Producer. The office was on the 14th floor of a glass tower resembling the building from *Die Hard* that was built uncomfortably close to the Christchurch Cathedral in downtown Montreal. I showed up in a shirt and tie with a briefcase full of CVs, a VHS demo tape, and a broad, happy, positive smile. The unfriendly woman at the front desk brought me to the boss without saying more than two words. Sitting at the desk was Donny. The stocky, late middle-aged man wore a short-sleeve button-down collared shirt with a bow tie and suspenders. Not only did he resemble Ted Kennedy, all red, round, large-headed and puffy, with his exact haircut, but the walls of his office were adorned with framed pictures of JFK and Jackie O. Before him were piles of papers stacked so high he was almost completely protected by a mini fort. He couldn't be bothered to look up at me.

"You wanna work on my shows?" he asked.

"Yes, sir," I said, reaching for a CV. "You can see that I am qualified …"

"You know where the Mount Stephen Club is, kid?"

"I … think I do."

"7 am Saturday. Don't be late," was all he said. "Give your info to my secretary."

I thanked him and after a moment of awkward silence, I rose and offered him my hand. He peered up with an annoyed glance and without standing, quickly took my hand and shook it, then went back to his papers. I gave his secretary my name and phone number and made my exit, making sure I kept my mouth shut so as not ruin this chance.

That was too *easy*, I thought.

The following Saturday I went downtown with my car, a brown late-model Chevy Celebrity sedan. The Mount Stephen Club was an old social gathering spot for wealthy English-speaking people located on Drummond Street. The grand, picturesque building, built in the late 1800s, was often used for movie locations or wedding receptions. There was one room in particular that was completely paneled in wood and visually stunning with amazing acoustics, making it ideal for filming. Keen and experienced Montreal driver that I was, I knew a street not far from there where, if I arrived early enough, I could park for free all day on weekends.

I gave my name to the Production Manager, a paid employee, and she was expecting me. I was immediately put to work unloading sandbags, lights, poles, and hernia-inducing power cables, which to this day remain the heaviest things I've had to carry. The interns were doing the grunt work, which I had anticipated. Hill and the other compensated employees were occupied with clerical and logistical tasks. The tapings lasted until about 5 pm. The interns were not given food or breaks, but there was "free" coffee; as in, "free" if you were able to sneak a cup when they weren't looking. As if to rub it in, it was the interns who were sent to pick up sandwiches and drinks for the paid crew, and when it was over we had to load the gear back into the trucks.

The day ran long and we were leaving late, just as guests for a wedding reception were arriving. They were upset we were still there. The paid staffers (with the exception of Hill) were unapologetic and, I found, a little rude to them. When the bride asked who was in charge, Donny came forward and yelled at her a series of profanities that almost made her cry. The crew, already quite aware of his temper, scattered. I stood stunned, then caught on, lowered my head, and kept moving the gear.

The next taping was two weeks later. Once again I showed up on time, ready to do any task assigned me, whether it was lifting heavy objects, lifting even heavier objects, or lifting practically immovable objects.

At one point I saw Donny chewing out the Production Manager. She had neglected to secure the taxi credit chits to get the guests from their hotel to the taping and back.

"What are you, a retard?" he said to her in front of the crew. "What the fuck are we supposed to do now?"

"I … I'm sorry Donny," she said, almost crying.

"Sorry!?! Well, I'm sorry I ever hired you!" he said. What made it worse was Donny was the kind of guy who spit when he talked, especially when he yelled, which was often, and the Production Manager was getting spritzed like a passenger on the Maid of the Mist II.

"I have a car," I said.

They quickly turned to me.

"What?" Donny said.

"I have a car. A sedan. I could get them for you."

"Good. Do that," Donny said, as his mood instantly changed. He turned to the Production Manager. "Make sure you pay him for his gas. Put his name in the end credits, too."

So I spent the day shuttling guests to and from the taping, picking them up at a hotel, the train station, and even the airport. In most cases, they were people I had heard of: Journalists, TV correspondents, and politicians.

I had educated myself so I wouldn't end up like my dad driving people around for a living, and now I was at last working in TV, driving people around, but *not* getting paid, so it was like being downwardly mobile.

They let me park my car in the back of the club. At the end of my day, I returned to give the Production Manager my gas receipt, only to find Hill there alone, crying.

"What's wrong?" I said.

"Donny, like, said he would pay me and he totally hasn't so far. When I went to him to ask why he called me an ungrateful bitch! So I quit."

"That asshole!" I said. "Y'know what? Fuck him, I'm quitting too …"

"No!" she said. "Please don't. It could harm your career. You need to do this. Don't worry, I'm totally fine. Fuck him. He's an asshole. I'm going home."

She got in her car and drove away. I stood there wondering what the hell I was in for with this. It was a moral dilemma: Should I stay loyal to my friend, or risk ruining my potential career in broadcasting?

That week I watched all the shows I had worked on and I did not see my name in the credits, nor did they compensate me for my gas.

The next production day they had me driving again. I didn't ask why they forgot the taxi vouchers this time. I didn't have to; I think they saw me as an exploitable commodity and an inexpensive car service.

They told me to drive one of the Production Assistants to Steve's Music Store, at the time on St. Antoine Street, to buy a mic stand. He had just had a confrontation with Donny that left him agitated. I tried to make small talk but that only served to further annoy him. I foolishly said that what he was going through would be worth it because he is working in the TV industry.

"Fuck TV, and fuck Donny! I'm not doing this for him. It's for me. I'm through doing anything for him! Let me give you some advice, kid," he said, despite being at least five years younger than me. "Don't ever do anything for him! He's an unappreciative rat bastard!"

"At least he could give you a reference," I said.

"Ha! Donny doesn't take reference calls or give recommendations. He's just an asshole. A total fucking, cocksucking, asshole!"

It was an uncharacteristically warm, sunny day in November. Later that afternoon during a break in the production I was sitting outside when I caught sight of a renowned Montreal author who had previously been on several of Donny's discussion group shows slowly making his way down Drummond Street. When I went in and told Donny that the author was outside he jumped out of his seat and ran directly to him, shaking his hand enthusiastically and smiling broadly, totally kissing his ass. The author appeared unimpressed and annoyed with the boot-licking clown and was soon on his way leaving Donny standing there, his face returning to his default scowl.

At the end of the day, an intern and I were tasked with getting a tape containing one of the shows to the airport so it could be sent to Toronto in time for airing that evening on CBC News Network. We had twenty minutes; a difficult task. I sped as quickly as I could, running yellow lights and dangerously weaving through traffic, but we were there five minutes too late. The plane left without the tape.

When I got back Donny berated me. "I'm not paying you to mess things up!" he said.

I had feelings of anger and guilt, so I just took the abuse and didn't shoot back with, "Well, you're not paying me at all!" like I should have. I was having my face fed to me without compensation. And at the end of the day, I didn't give in my gas receipts for fear I'd get chewed out again.

I wanted to quit, but I was committed to five more taping dates that year; a commitment I fulfilled even though they consistently failed to compensate me for my gas or so much as put my name in the credits once, in any of the shows. When I completed the last date of that calendar year, my final assignment was to drive one of the hosts, a veteran TV journalist and news anchor, to the airport. He asked me what it was like working with Donny. I said, "It's like dancing with a chainsaw." He smiled and said that sounded about right.

The TV Journalist regaled me with interesting and amusing insider anecdotes where he pulled no punches. I recounted to him the time I went to Toronto and tried to get a job on a morning program and the disaster that ensued when I accidentally informed the host that he was being replaced before the show's producer did.

"Yeah," the TV Journalist said, laughing, "That's how they do things there."

The following January the shows were to start production again. I came home from the record store to find a message on my machine from the Production Manager, requesting my services for the new series of tapings. She asked for the correct spelling of my name to put it in the credits and said that I should give her my receipts for gas so I could be paid, even though I had already given her all of them. I didn't call back. I figured it wouldn't hurt me. Donny didn't learn my name. No one there did.

* * *

More than a dozen years later I was producing a literary event when I ran into Donny, now elderly and walking with the help of a cane. He came to speak to one of the authors at the event, a famous and powerful magazine editor with a new book to promote, with whom he claimed he was friends. I don't know what Donny wanted to talk to him about but the editor was annoyed with his presence and blew him off.

I went up to Donny afterward and told him I had worked on his shows in the late 90s, but he had absolutely no recollection of me just like I had predicted. He asked for my card and said he had a business idea he would like to throw past me.

"Sure. We'll talk about it. May I have *your* card, please?" I asked.

He did. His office address was now residential. Phone number looked like a cell.

I didn't call him.

He telephoned me a number of times, once leaving an almost incomprehensible, meandering message on my voicemail where he dropped Gore Vidal's name, but I avoided the calls and did not reply. He eventually caught me at work and I asked him to email me his proposal. What he sent was, like his phone messages, short on practical details, and certain parts made no sense. I don't know what I would've done were his plan remotely feasible, but fortunately for me it was not. What he wanted demonstrated no knowledge of book retail and how literary events work and why bookstores have them, so I emailed a terse but polite "no" around a week later. He called me back a few times and I was able to put him off with a "we'll see," but I didn't contact him again and after a while he stopped trying to reach me.

I thought doing that to him would give me some degree of satisfaction. I was surprised to find it didn't. It just left me feeling empty and shallow. Sure, he was a total douche. But how did my acting like just as big a douche make it right?

Five years later I came across him walking down the street wearing clothes that looked like they were once pricey but were now old, well-worn, and out of style. He gave off an air of trying to keep up appearances and dignity, but was fighting a hopeless battle. He looked unsure of his time and place. I walked right past him and nodded in his direction. He nodded back but his facial expression was one of puzzlement. He didn't know who I was.

While there is no excuse for the abusive things he said to Hill and other staffers, I couldn't help but think about how I didn't know who he really was. By then Gore Vidal was gone. Did he have other friends? Were *they* still alive? Did he have a family? Was he loved? Did he sacrifice all that for his career, one that is no longer there and forgotten by most?

I watched him walk away and an uneasy feeling came over, that one day I could be him. We all could.

I DON'T SHARE DAIRY

What do Pat Benatar, Ray Romano, Hulk Hogan, Will Ferrell, and I have in common?

We all, at one point in our lives, worked as bank tellers.

When I say that I worked as a bank teller people inevitably ask if I've been in a holdup. And I was. On my first day. At my wicket. I look back on that now as an omen.

My first few years in high finance are most notable for being the longest period where my love life consisted of nothing but first dates. Not sure why that was so, but it was an interesting time.

During my tenure at a branch across from the airport I earned a reputation for being a bit of a character. So much so that one client took to calling me Regis because I reminded her of TV personality Regis Philbin, whose game show *Who Wants to be a Millionaire?* was popular at the time. (Seldom does anyone say to me something like, "You are just like Sean Connery" or someone cool like that. No, they say things like, "You bring to mind Eddie Deezen.")

Around then we transferred in a new teller to replace one that was being promoted. She was friends with Helga, a stocky, self-described biker chick, who was the veteran teller that occupied the wicket next to mine. The new teller was sort of a Stevie Nicks type, so I will call her Stevie. She worked on the other side of my station. We were all about the same age and the three of us soon became a fun trio; each day we worked together was like a small party.

One snowy, powerfully cold Friday evening we finished work and went to our respective cars. I was waiting for my vehicle to warm up when there was an unexpected knock on my car window. It was Stevie.

"Can I come in?" she asked.

"Sure," I said, unlocking my car doors. She slid into the passenger seat.

Her SUV was parked across from me. According to her, it took forever for her vehicle to properly warm up, and she lived off-island so she wanted to wait for the traffic on the Mercier Bridge to clear.

We started talking and laughing and enjoying each other's company. She left after about twenty minutes, saying she had to make supper for her daughter and partner.

The next Friday we did the same thing again, but this time we discussed heavier subjects. She spoke about how she was no longer happy with her current boyfriend, who was not the father of her daughter, and felt the relationship would soon be over.

It became a regular thing for us, even when it was no longer cold. I had the feeling that she wanted to avoid going home. By late spring she told me she had decided to leave her boyfriend, and eventually she and her daughter moved out of his house. A few Fridays after that when we sat talking, she grabbed my hand and held it tightly as we engaged in sparkling conversation.

Our Branch Manager by then was an affable woman named Charlene. She was a career teller who was abruptly given a branch to command and I must say she did an excellent job. She kept her composure no matter what was going on, and if she had a problem with an employee she would quietly call them into her office and talk civilly to them like they were a human being. Charlene did not belittle anyone and we all enjoyed working under her. She was especially impressed with my knowledge of our clients and how friendly and personable I was with all of them

Until an unfortunate incident.

There was a regular customer (I will call him Mr. Johnson … not his real name) who came in one day when it was busy and ended up at my wicket. He withdrew $2000 cash in hundreds and quickly left. A few days later I was called into Charlene's office and asked if I knew what "kiting" was.

"That is when a person deposits a bad check in the cash machine and then withdraws the money before it bounces. Why do you ask?"

"Was it you who served Mr. Johnson a few days ago?" she said. I wasn't sure why Charlene asked if she already knew. There was no way for me to deny it. "Well, the $2000 he took out was from a cheque he deposited a few minutes earlier in our machine. The cheque was no good."

"When something like that happens the branch has to pay for it. It comes out of our bonuses. Here." She pushed a paper towards me. "Sign this taking the responsibility. You will not get a bonus this year."

I looked at the paper, and up at Charlene. Her eyes had lost their smile and she reeked of anxiety. I read what was written on the paper.

"I want to think about this," I said. "Can I have a few minutes alone?"

"Just sign it."

"I have the right to think about it, don't I?"

"Sure."

I went to the staff room and grabbed my cellphone and a cigarette, and ran out of the branch, immediately calling The Weasel.

"C'mon, pick up! Please, please pick up!" I said to myself.

For once he answered.

"What's up?" he said. I explained the situation. Because he managed his own branch, he had access to all the pertinent information. After a minute or two that felt like an hour or four, he said, "Do *NOT* sign that! No matter what! They can't make you. They're trying to set you up! Mr. Johnson's accounts are at another branch. They issued him a card with no holds on deposits up to $10,000. The only limit was to how much he could withdraw at one time at the ATM. He put in a cheque for $3500, took out his cash limit, $1500, at the machine and went to you for the other $2000. You had no reason to refuse him. There were no messages on his account at the time. It is all on the other branch. I know the manager there, he's a shrewd guy. Charlene is inexperienced and he's probably trying to get her to take the rap. He has to absorb the $1500 from the machine, no way around that. But he's trying to screw Charlene. Do not sign it, and tell her what I told you: it should go to the other branch. Don't let them do this to you. They could fire you if you sign that paper!"

"Why would he do that? The guy is a long-time client in good standing. A grandfather, even!"

"Who knows?" The Weasel said. "I've seen it a million times. Gambling. Drinking. Hookers. Drugs. Whatever? I've had clients end up murdered, their bodies discovered in the trunk of their cars. Sometimes people get in over their heads. That doesn't matter. Just don't sign!"

I went back and stood my ground with Charlene. Our bank was on the verge of a corporate merger with another. I knew that. But what The Weasel and I did not know at the time was, as a result of that, Charlene was being transferred to the other branch, the one where Mr. Johnson had his accounts. And she didn't want all of the $3500 waiting for her. Charlene was the shrewd one in this case. So she absorbed the $2000 at our branch, and when she eventually left and the new boss came in, he found it $2000 in the hole. And when he asked who was responsible, guess what happened.

The new General Manager, a West-Island WASP, was furious with me right out of the gate. (I visited my father around the time this was happening. When he asked me what the new manager was like, I asked him if he watched *Frasier*. When he said he did, I said he reminded me of his brother Niles. Dad laughed so hard he almost swallowed his cigarette.)

Niles didn't care much for the way I worked and didn't dig my gregarious personality even though the customers did, so when it was decided by head office we were going to be folded into another branch in the same area, he saw that as an ample opportunity to alleviate himself of my presence. As well, Niles decided to get rid of Helga despite the fact that when he first started working with the bank she was the one who trained him as a teller. She took this as a chance to expand her horizons, and a year later when the merger happened she accepted a compensation deal which, because of her over fifteen years' service, was quite generous, and moved on to better things.

I was able to secure a position at a primarily commercial branch on Decarie Boulevard in the TMR industrial park. I kept up my friendships with Helga and Stevie. In fact, after I left, Stevie took to calling me at home on Friday nights and we would have long, often deeply personal conversations.

After she had been single for a few months I felt it was now acceptable to ask her on a date, and, in what to me was a pleasant surprise, she said "yes." We agreed on a day and time and when it arrived she stood me up.

Sadly, this was not the first or last time something like that happened to me. I was aware of the protocol and didn't ask her out or try to speak to her again. For a while, anyway.

Stevie stopped calling me at home. Helga telephoned me one day at work for an unrelated professional matter. When we finished she said, "Stevie wants to say 'hi' to you!"

"Sure," I said with a Cheshire Cat grin, "put her on."

"Hi, Andreas!" she said.

"You stood me up!" I said, in clear violation of etiquette. (But it felt good to be able to say that for once.)

"I have an excuse," she said.

"What?" I said. "What's your excuse?"

"Well, I was sorta busy ..."

"You stood me up!"

"Sorry," she said, handing the phone back to a giggling Helga, who overheard what I had said.

A few weeks later the three of us met for drinks at a run-down roadhouse biker bar under a highway on the West Island. We laughed about the whole thing and remain friends to this day.

One of the clients at my new branch was a record company. Francine from their accounts receivable department (in truth, I think she *was* the accounts receivable department) made their deposits and did their banking. She had thick, curly-brown hair, cheerful blue eyes, and a warm, friendly smile. It was not too long after my stint at a record store, and it turned out she used to work at one as well, in her case the Sam's downtown; a cool and well-renowned establishment. We even had some friends in common. Occasionally she would bring me a free CD.

One summer day Francine came by to make a deposit and waited for my wicket to be available. She said she had tickets to a show at the Metropolis (as the theatre was called at the time, before being tagged with a heartless corporate moniker) on Ste. Catherine Street that night and asked if I wanted to go with her. I said yes.

We met at the Park Avenue Metro Station and took the 80 bus downtown. It was the first time I had seen her without being behind a teller's window. Our conversation was continuous but she was a little distant and uneasy; less bubbly than she was at the bank. I wasn't sure if it was something I said or did or if there was another factor of which I was unaware.

At the concert, we kept running into people she knew and she spoke to them with what was clearly more enthusiasm. In fact, she spent most of our time there in conversation with other people and ignoring me.

After the show, we walked to the Dairy Queen on Park Avenue. She avoided looking at me and I felt like I wasn't her first choice for a date that night, which ultimately turned out to be the case; she had recently broken up with someone else.

At the D.Q. we ordered different items. She was enjoying hers and I asked if I could try some.

"I don't share dairy," she said.

The line was silly and I thought she was just kidding with me so I asked again in a playful manner, reaching over with my plastic spoon. She shot me an angry look as she jerked her cup out of my reach.

"I said I don't share dairy! What the hell is wrong with you?"

We parted where we began the night at the Park Avenue metro station. Someone else started coming for the record company bank deposits, and by Christmas I had transferred to the bank's credit card division.

Marianne Cortes was tall and slender and wore glasses that were the perfect size, shape, and colour to accentuate her Brazilian/German features.

When she made deposits for the company that employed her we would often exchange small talk. I learned she was in a committed relationship and was an amateur photographer. We got along well and we shared a similar sense of humour, but I didn't think more of it until the day she went out of her way to make sure I was her teller.

Upon arriving at my wicket the first thing she did was ask for my phone number. I was unsure why. Before I could even stamp her cheques she asked if I had any plans for that night.

Why does she suddenly want to see me socially? I asked myself. *Was my luck changing? No ... There had to be something else. I just don't get this lucky.*

I once had a client call me at home after looking up my number in the phone book. They wanted me to un-deposit a cheque they had given me at work. I informed them that I didn't bring the cheque home with me and that it was already on the way to a clearing house. Then I told them not to call me again outside of work and hung up the phone. I wondered if this was something similar. Maybe she wanted to discuss a financial issue of some kind? Perhaps she wanted a loan? Or a job with the bank?

Marianne and I quickly set up a date for that evening and I gave her my addresses, both residential and email. She insisted on driving and avoided giving me her phone number, or any contact info other than an email address.

My Spidey-senses continued to tingle. There was something amiss.

But what could it be?

Marianne picked me up on time and we ventured to St. Denis Street to find an eatery. On our way there she asked if I had checked my email. When I told her no she said that she had sent me some samples of her photography.

While we were perusing the various restaurant menu displays she made her intentions pretty clear: She aggressively grabbed my arm and pulled herself close to me. I began mentioning places I had been to before and she said in a jealous manner, "I don't want to hear about where you brought your other dates!" All that did was make me more suspicious.

Why was she instantly so affectionate and possessive? Did she break up with her boyfriend and I was the rebound guy? Or were things about to start going my way?

Dare to fucking dream.

We agreed to dine at a nice pub that coincidentally used to be a bank. It was a little too dark inside for my taste but was quiet enough and the atmosphere was good for conversation.

I asked Marianne about herself. She told me that she was born into a cult headquartered in rural Quebec. Her parents were long-time members. I was mesmerized by her tale; it was interesting and she told it well. Moreover, it explained some of the elements of her quirky personality. I started to loosen up and get comfortable. My suspicions slowly began to melt away and I was having a great time.

I don't remember how or why but we started to discuss *Powder*, a movie about a teenager with telekinetic abilities that she had seen recently. She said Johnny Depp was really good in the film.

"I haven't seen it, but I know it isn't Johnny Depp in the lead, it's another actor. I can't remember his name, but I'm certain of it," I said. She continued to insist that it was Depp.

After dinner, she turned serious and asked, "You're probably wondering why I asked you out tonight?"

"Yes, the thought had sort of crossed my mind," I said. Then I asked, "Didn't you say once you have a steady guy?"

"Well," she said, "I did. But we broke up. You see, there is this six-unit triplex in St. Sauveur that is going for an unbelievable, once-in-a-lifetime price. We wanted to buy it, but when we went to the bank for a mortgage it turns out that not only did he not have any money, but he owed a lot all over town. You see he drove a BMW and had a Rolex watch. He had a good job and earned a good salary, but he spent a lot as well and he didn't tell me about his financial problems. He is such a fucking liar! So I dumped him. Look, if we get the place we could live together in one of the apartments and the rents from the other five units should cover the mortgage, insurance, and then some. It's a great place in great condition. I know you'll love it!"

I could clearly hear the distinct, sadly familiar, and unsurprising clunk of the other shoe dropping.

In the banking business, we are privy to our clients' financial secrets. It was not uncommon for the jerk with the BMW (it's often a BMW or Mercedes, but now Audi, Range Rover, and Tesla are closing in fast), and the fancy threads to have an empty bank account because they spend money as if loonies rained from the heavens, while the old guy in the beat-up Chevy Malibu, the tacky polyester clothes bought at Walmart, and the bad comb-over, was invariably the actual millionaire.

I saw the enthusiasm drain from her eyes as I began to sink into my seat like a slowly deflating balloon. In my head, I said to myself, *You idiot! An attractive woman interested in* you*? What were you thinking? Did you really think that she liked you? Get two forms of I.D. and cash a reality check, Kessaris!*

I told her that my salary as a teller was not all that high, I had little in my savings and was a bit in debt myself. In fact, my tenure working for one of the largest corporations in Canada was the poorest and most indebted era of my life so far. I had $2000 overdraft protection on my chequing account, and I was living in that overdraft at the time and didn't get my balance above sea level for years. As an employee, I was entitled to a better mortgage rate, but I didn't have enough money to put down a deposit on real estate, and certainly didn't qualify for such a large loan, even if it was with someone else. Nothing was automatic. I then pointed out how we hardly knew each other and a life-altering long-term decision like what she was proposing shouldn't be approached so irresponsibly. Who knew if we would get along?

Her mood instantly changed. She became angry with me as if I had deceived her as well.

We hardly spoke on the ride home. When I asked why she was so secretive about her phone number and why she would not let me pick her up, she told me she had a daughter. She was married in the cult at eighteen and now had a teenage daughter. I was floored. Helga can't go five minutes without mentioning one of her two daughters, and now her granddaughter, yet Marianne told me her life story and did not mention her former marriage or offspring once. When was she going to tell me? When we moved in together did she think I wouldn't notice there was a fourteen-year-old girl living with us?

She dropped me off at my front door and said a sour "thanks for dinner" as she drove off the moment I exited her vehicle.

When I got home I went straight to the internet to check on who the lead in *Powder* was and in fact it was Sean Patrick Flanery and not Johnny Depp as she had said. I opened my email and found what Marianne had sent me. Her photos consisted of images of animals found on the side of the road crushed by cars. And that's how I felt at that moment: like a dead raccoon on the highway. I still sent her the message about *Powder*, but she didn't reply.

Marianne avoided my wicket from then on. When she came by the branch she didn't look in my direction and if my eyes veered towards her, she would sneer at me contemptuously.

What did *I* do? I'm still not sure. I wasn't the dishonest one, no matter how you looked at it.

* * *

One Saturday afternoon years later, while riding my bike back from the Olympic Stadium, I ran into Francine.

We talked, and I told her about how, on a recent trip to Ontario where I visited my old college buddy Rick and his family, I recounted to them the story of our ill-fated date, and how the whole "I don't share dairy" thing ended up becoming our catch-phrase for the weekend.

Misunderstanding my intentions and taking what I said to be an insult, Francine became offended and said to me, "Well if you wanted the ice cream so badly I could have just spooned some into yours, you jerk!" and stormed off.

Serves me right for stopping.

SACKED

It was a warm June morning. I sat on a bench outside the Sherbrooke Street glass edifice where I was once employed, with a brown file box atop my lap. I had loosened my tie, unbuttoned my collar, and I continued to sit there because I didn't know what else to do. I had never been fired before.

I'm not a fan of that word. "Fired." Too harsh. Too mean. Too violent. I prefer the British term "sacked." It's a bit lighter. Funnier, even; not so terrible or final, like "terminated." I first came across it while watching the opening credits of a Monty Python movie. I was young and didn't know what it meant, but Peter explained it to me by saying, "That's what the English say instead of 'fired'." You imagine a person hearing the news, shrugging, packing their things in a sack, slinging it over their shoulder, and walking away into the sunset in a Chaplinesque, happy-go-lucky manner. You don't feel as bad getting "sacked" as you would "fired." That's where I was, ready to walk away into the sunset, except holding a cardboard box by the handles. Unfortunately it was not yet 10 am, and the setting sun was a ways off.

People who walked past, if they noticed me at all, probably gathered that I had my ass handed to me and now I was one step away from the gutter, which lay at me feet.

How did I get here? Kept going through my head.

How did *I get here*?

* * *

My employment history has been rather unorthodox. From a young age, I knew I would have to get a job in order to pay my way through life. When I was six or seven I saw a man on TV who worked on a factory assembly line gluing soles onto the bottom of shoes. I figured that could be my vocation. I have arms and hands. I can do the gig. Easy enough. I even imagined myself married with a family, and when we had guests over and they asked what I did for a living, I'd say I glued shoes together, and then point to their feet and say, "Hey! I did those shoes!" and they'd be impressed.

As I grew older I realized I had the potential to aim a little higher than shoe gluer, not that I'm implying that there is something wrong with that; it's an honest living. Lots of good, respectable people work assembly lines.

At fifteen I had a part-time summer job at an ice factory owned by a friend of my father. My mom got me my second part-time gig, this time at a bakery, the next summer. Both minimum wage and both perfect for a teenager, although one was too cold, the other too hot.

At seventeen I was in Old Montreal with some friends, headed to an arcade to play the game *Final Lap* when we happened upon a movie set, a common sight in that area. American productions often film there because of its European feel, but when Montrealers see those movies and it's supposed to be London, Paris or Moscow, we just laugh. They had wrapped for the day and I started chatting with one of the crew members. I asked if he knew how I can get work as an extra, and he told me of a place. I went the following day and throughout my college and university days, I worked as an extra for film and TV productions. I helped liberate France from the Nazis, was a protesting racist farmer, a preppy college student, a guy in a suit who strolls past Donald Sutherland and Helen Mirren, and one of three thugs who beat up an old man … and then there was my work in films! Seriously though, the work paid well for what was asked of me, especially if there was a costume call, and the flexible hours were a perfect fit for a student, but the jobs were infrequent and I needed a means of making more money.

When I graduated College I had, at the time, no plans to go on to university; my generation saw CEGEP as a respectable achievement. I tried to find work in TV and film after a fruitful run at Dawson's Cinema/Communications department, but had little luck and my mom felt that I needed to get going in my life, so she called in a favour from her baby brother, a prosperous restaurateur, and asked if he could help me get started on a career. My uncle was not the proprietor of a hot dog stand or pizzeria. He owned a high-end, elegant steakhouse and strip mall on the South Shore. He had four daughters who were not interested in the family business and no sons, so he agreed to take me on as a possible successor. He came to Canada with nothing, and through his sweat, ambition and determination became a completely self-made man in what is a true Horatio Alger story. And he'd be the first one to tell you that. The reality was that, while my uncle was hard-working and dedicated his life to his business, my mom had helped him out by lending him $500 in the late 60s so he could open his first eatery, a debt he quickly paid back once his restaurant took off. He had a large, framed sign in his office that read, "No Smoking! I probably enjoy sex more than you enjoy cigarettes. I don't fuck in your office, so you don't smoke in mine!"

Classy!

My father, who remained close to his ex-brother-in-law, drove me to his establishment one afternoon and we had coffee. Years earlier they were hunting buddies, and they had a strong mutual respect, despite my father being a communist and my uncle a venture capitalist.

My uncle sat us down in his steakhouse dining room and gathered himself together before giving his pitch. He spoke about how much he loved the restaurant game and what it had given him. There was a passion in his words that surprised me. His line of work involved long hours and little personal time, so one had to love it, but I didn't know if I could, and I knew that if I didn't I would be miserable most of the time.

"You mother told me," he said, "that you want to work *een* TV, radio or film. Why? What do you like about that?"

"Well, I enjoy working with a team of people toward a goal," I said. "Getting together, exchanging ideas, working on a project, and seeing it come to life. I like entertaining people, and making them happy."

"The restaurant business *eez* exactly that," my uncle said. "It *eez* like show business. Every night *eez* like the opening of a show. You have a team here that *eez* creative. The food *eez* the show. You entertain people. You make them happy. You be a *celebritee*."

At the time I thought what he said was pretty lame. Now I can see that he was right; chefs and restaurateurs are now famous, although to this day I don't regret turning him down. I respect that career path. It just wasn't for me.

During my higher education days, there were a number of elections on all three levels of government, and my father, well-connected with politicians, found me work registering voters, as a ballot taker, and in various clerical jobs with electoral offices. Once again the pay was good, but once again the jobs were infrequent.

Dad had set up for me a summer gig on an assembly line at a T-shirt factory one year, but my first steady, year-round employment was courtesy of my brother's then-girlfriend Annick, who hired me without so much as an interview as a service station attendant, which I eventually did at three different locations for about a year and a half. Despite it being mostly waiting around it was a real job, for a person has not truly worked until they've had to clean a toilet to which a careless and inconsiderate public has access.

I worked weekends at the station in NDG for a summer while at University. The owner/manager was a guy named Chuck. He would give us our paychecks and then tell us to endorse the back, return them to him, and extract our money out of the cash register. One week my pay was $89.43. When he noticed I was pulling the exact amount to the penny from the till Chuck yelled at me, "What are you, a Jew!?!" That's all one needs to know about the kind of guy he was.

During Labour Day weekend Chuck went away with his family and neglected to raise the price of gas, as was often done during peak times. (I was told by Chuck that all stations set their prices by territory to ensure no real competition, which I thought was illegal, but what do I know?) I worked Friday to Monday and it was non-stop. I did not have even a moment to go to the washroom. The District Rep from our company called in a furious rage and demanded that I raise the price. I told her the assistant manager of the station was not answering his phone and Chuck was in Quebec City, and I wasn't trained how to make the changes, but if they sent someone over to do it I would assist them any way I could.

"We are doing great business! What's the big deal?" I said to them.

The Rep, whom I had met a few times before and was so warm and pleasant, cursed me out in French before calling me useless, slamming down the phone, and I can only assume violently pulling said unit out of the wall and throwing it across the room. Mostly a cash business at the time, I kept dropping deposits in the floor safe until it couldn't take anymore.

What I didn't know at the time was that the other stations in the area, our "competition," complained like all hell was breaking loose to our head office for violating the sacred covenant and not raising our prices to match theirs, and now it all fell on The Rep, who would probably get chewed out by their boss on Tuesday.

Late Monday afternoon Chuck drove up to empty the safe. I told him what had transpired and all about the phone call from The Rep but he waved me off and hardly said a word. He took a huge bag and emptied the safe. Then he, in what was a breach of procedure, took the bag home with him. I thought nothing of it, really.

That Fall another NDG station with the same oil company had its franchise revoked because the owner cheated on a contest. We were to pass scratch cards out to our customers with each sale of 25 litres or more for a chance to win a new car. They had their employees scratch all the tickets they were given for distribution until they found a winner. Then the owner sent a relative to collect the car, thinking for some reason that head office was brain-dead and wouldn't notice. So the company gave Chuck that station and I was transferred there. It was a small, enclosed place on a sleazy street known for its prostitutes, and I believed it was banishment to Siberia, although I was unsure as to what rule I had broken.

I worked that Christmas and New Year's, both the eves and the days and other holidays, two weeks full time to cover for the other employees who unlike myself had loved ones to be with, and I was glad to do so. I would be paid time-and-a-half and was waiting for a windfall that did not arrive. It turns out Chuck had purloined the aforementioned Labour Day loot for himself. He was at the bank doing business one afternoon just before he took all the cash home when his teller walked away. He reached over the counter, took her stamp, and endorsed a blank page in his record book. A while later he faked a huge cash deposit. (What kind of people were they giving franchises to? Would-be criminals who believe they are masterminds?) So I had new bosses, but they were under no obligation to give Chuck's employees their due. I lost the best two-weeks salary I had earned in my life at that point. I called the head office, but they didn't care. I sold their products and wore a uniform with their logo. I did their training. I even have a diploma from their customer service school. I did all they asked of me. A huge multi-national conglomerate and they refused to give me a measly (for them) two weeks' pay. All I wanted was what I was owed. No more, no less. I went to the press, to the government, to any organization that could do something, and made formal complaints but they all came to nothing. Chuck had filed for bankruptcy protection, so I didn't get a cent of what I had earned. I worked until the spring, and after having exhausted all avenues, quit in disgust. I just couldn't work for them anymore.

My next steady payroll job was in 1994. I had just earned my degree, ending more than twenty years of school from pre-k to university, and I vowed not to return to any educational institute again. I was twenty-four and it was time I got my life going. But what now? I had to find work. I had debts I needed to address so I moved back in with my mother to work out my financial situation. She had just divorced her second husband and had two extra rooms in her new flat.

I printed out CVs and went around to television or radio stations, as well as newspapers and production companies, to no avail. I had a two-week gig at the beginning of the summer at the election office bureau of revisions that made me a few bucks, so I had enough cash to last the summer. (Although I was living with Mom, I still had to pay my share of the bills.)

The Weasel joined the chorus and got on my case to find a job as well. I don't know if he was jealous that I had the summer off or was concerned for my future (probably a little bit of both, and a lot of neither). I had given him a handful of my CVs and told him to give them out to any of his bank clients who were in the arts or entertainment industry and looking for workers, ignorant of the fact that gigs like that were rare, impermanent, and did not pay well.

One day The Weasel called and invited me to the mall where he worked for lunch on him.

You bet! One of my goals in life is to prove that yes, there is such a thing as a free lunch. My Latin motto should be "I Si Non Sapiunt I!"

When I showed up, The Weasel had one of my CVs in his hand. He gave it to me and led the way to a record store that had opened the day before, introduced me to the assistant manager, a guy named Chris P., and told him I was looking for work. I handed him the CV and shook his hand. Then we went to eat, which was more interesting to me.

A few weeks later I was called by that assistant manager, and was soon interviewed and employed. I thought the gig would last until I found a better job (which didn't come). So I avoided taking the work too seriously. Sure I showed up on time and did what I was told, but I was guilty of goofing off from time to time and joking around incessantly.

Chris P. took me aside one day and told me point blank that if I didn't stop my antics he would have to fire me. The customers and my co-workers had had enough of me and he was tired of taking complaints.

"You're a good guy, Andreas, and not a bad worker when you're on top of things," he said, "but you are also an incredible flake. Now the full-time position is opening up, and if you want it you have to get it together. I know you are only here until you find a career job, but believe me, the attitude you have here is the attitude you will carry through your professional life. Right now if someone asked for a reference I couldn't tell them that you were a good employee."

It occurred to me at that moment: One of the reasons I was hired was because The Weasel put in a good word for me, and now I was letting him down and making Chris P., who was poised to become manager of another store in the chain, look like a chump. I took what he said to heart, and appreciated his honesty. This was not the gas station, where I spent my time trying to get away with doing as little as possible. I had to get it together, and I did, earning the promotion to full-time.

When Chris P. left he was replaced by a guy named Gord, a short, bitter, underachiever with a hair-trigger temper. Add to that he was sexist, racist, and anti-gay, and there you had the complete package. He stole products from the store and was generally dishonest. If one were to look up the word "unpleasant" in the dictionary, his picture would be there. Once he had the hots for a customer, a pretty blonde named Kim. He was smitten and gave her deals on CDs and movies, if not for free. Then one day she came into the store, hand in hand with her boyfriend, who was not only handsome and rich, but decidedly not Gord. And he was surprised? Was he the only person in the world who didn't realize that she wouldn't fuck a troll like him? I had by then given him the moniker "The Jittery Jerk" behind his back. In keeping with his character, he completely lost it the moment they left, hopping around like a caged monkey, taking it out on all of us, causing one employee to quit on the spot. When he acted like that I would play the song "You Jerk" by Kim Stockwood in the store. It gave me a smile and a snicker, especially because Gord didn't seem catch on to the reason why I spun that ditty.

I used to smoke in those days and when I did in the back room of the store I would open the door to the service corridor to air out the place. One day I forgot to close it again and Gord went totally ballistic. Although he was right that it was a security issue, I felt he over-reacted when he wrote me an official reprimand that was sent to human resources at the head office in Toronto. I became worried that if a potential employer contacted them and asked if I had any black marks on my record it would come back to haunt me. Today the company is no more. I have had plenty of other work experience, and the only way anyone would know about it now is if they read this.

After a couple of years Gord quit for a better job and took his assistant manager with him. It wasn't long before they were both on the unemployment line again. Apparently it's not as easy to get away with shenanigans when more closely supervised. I became the assistant manager, and in time the manager of the store. When I was promoted I discovered that some of the tasks Gord and his assistant had assigned me, like weekly inventory and setting up complex displays and promotions, were, as defined by the company's operation manual (referred to as "The Bible"), strictly and exclusively to be done by management. Gord had even made me go out and get his lunch daily because he said that according to "The Bible" the manager wasn't permitted to leave the store during the day. I was fit to be tied when I found out it was bullshit all along.

Gord lived close to the store and would come by from time to time, like a black sheep showing up at a family gathering drunk and demanding pocket money, and ask if he could take a video or CD, which I would refuse. He sunk to an even deeper low when he approached The Weasel at his bank branch and asked him for a personal cash loan. When he refused, Gord fired at him: "You would lend Andreas money if he asked!" To which The Weasel replied, "We have known each other since we were fifteen. He was Best Man at my wedding! I don't know you at all!"

I ran into Gord a decade later. I shook his hand and said it was nice to see him. I felt so dirty. I told this to one of my former co-workers. She said she understood how I felt. The dirt still won't wash off, no matter how hard I scrub.

When I was named manager of the record store I was about to turn thirty and making less than $10 an hour in a business that was on the decline and soon to disappear altogether, due to the new technological innovations called "downloading" and "file sharing."

I was unhappy, and wanted more. I had abandoned all hope in trying to find employment in my field. With a half-dozen years of writing on the side I was still unpublished, my scripts unsold, and I was mired in debt. I needed a better job with a future, a livable wage, and benefits.

I talked to The Weasel about my woes one day and he told me he could get me an interview with the bank, which was looking to expand its in-branch customer service hours, so they needed people with my kind of work experience.

"I don't know, man, I can't really see myself at a bank," I said. "I'm not like you."

"Look, you work forty-two hours a week and make nothing. Wouldn't you rather work fewer hours for more money?" The Weasel said. "And you could have dental and prescription drug benefits. What does the store give you? Just glasses? And there are financial advantages as well, including low-interest loans and credit cards. More paid sick days. What have you got to lose?"

He had a point. On the one hand, while my pay sucked, and with few benefits other than free CDs, videos and posters, as well as potential free concert tickets (which not once did I get), I loved music and movies and the gig at least had something to do with my passions; on the other hand, I was getting older, in a serious relationship, and had still failed to launch into anything meaningful. So I took him up on his kind offer and not long afterward, just like he predicted, I was working fewer hours for more money and benefits.

My girlfriend at the time was ecstatic that I had finally landed a "real adult job" and was no longer wasting my time at a record store. (This was the same girlfriend who told me in a fit of anger to stop wasting my time trying to find a career in the arts. "Everyone I know in that business is struggling. Do you want to struggle your whole life?" she'd say to me.) She bought me a gift for my first day at the new place: A light-blue dress shirt and matching blue and gray striped tie. We broke up four months later. About a week or so after that I was browsing in the local Cohoes (a now-defunct discount clothing store) and saw on display the exact shirt and tie combo she had purchased for me, selling for $25. That really hurt. Worse, I was wearing the aforementioned combo at the time. The shirt lasted about two years, but I still have the tie. It's a nice tie; goes with a lot of my clothing.

I made the best of my new gig and did well. I got to know my customers and they liked my personality. One in particular was a senior named Mrs. Holmes. She was Austrian but married to an Englishman (a genuine one, from England) who was a total sourpuss. She, on the other hand, with her dainty little-old-lady clothes and constant smile, was so wonderful I enjoyed having her at my wicket.

Around holiday time Mrs. Holmes asked what my favourite candy bar was. I told her Snickers. The next day I started at noon and when I arrived the other tellers came up to me and said, "What did you do to Mrs. Holmes?"

I was unsure and a little worried. Did I do or say something to offend her? Did I make a mistake with her banking? It turned out she had come by in the morning with two bags of mini candy bars. One Mars, the other Snickers. (Around Christmas clients often brought us treats like candy and cookies.) She told them the Mars bars were for them but gave strict instructions that the Snickers bars were exclusively for me.

I saw Mrs. Holmes a few days later and thanked her, asking why she bought a bag just for me.

"Well, Andreas," she said with her pleasant accent, "young men seldom smile at old women. But you smile at me."

A few months later the slight and perpetually unhappy Mr. Holmes came into the bank early to deposit his pension cheque from the Royal Navy; a paltry amount, but he brought it in monthly the day it arrived in the mail. I asked how he was but the tight-lipped Brit stayed in character and did not reply; in fact, he appeared to be annoyed by me. I asked him if anything was new and he just harrumphed. Later that same day Mrs. Holmes passed by with the broadest smile. She had just come from the one-hour photo shop in the neighbouring mall with pictures of her new granddaughter, who was born the night before.

I was confused.

"Do you have other grandchildren?" I asked.

"No, this is our first!"

"Your husband, is this his grandchild as well?"

"Yes."

"He was here this morning," I said.

"Yes, I was in the car outside. I could not wait to go to the hospital, but he's always in a hurry to deposit that silly cheque."

"But … he was so … so … I asked him if anything was new and he … I mean … if it were my first grandchild I would be ecstatic … bouncing off the walls …"

"Andreas, the English," Mrs. Holmes said, "they are not like us. They don't show emotions."

I stayed at that branch for a year and a half, but I needed to make better money. Then the new manager gave me the old heave-ho. I found a position at a commercial branch where I worked full-time Monday to Friday and for the first time in my life I had weekends off. Most of the staff liked me, the tellers were a tight-knit group, and after a while I worked my way up to Lead Teller, a position of more responsibility that, despite the "Lead" part, did not give me augmented pay or any real authority.

My first manager of customer service, who was my immediate supervisor, was a bit of a busybody. If there were no clients in the branch she expected us to do other work, despite the fact that it was not part of our job description. She targeted me especially, and made me clean, which I wasn't supposed to do. The bank hired cleaning people to do that after hours. I filed a complaint with head office, which only made her hate me more. Fortunately, the customers didn't care for her as well so after a few months, she was moved to another branch. Her replacement appreciated my efforts and personality. I was happy and in all seriousness considered working there for the rest of my life.

In the bank, there are two kinds of bosses: good ones that leave after six months, and bad ones that endlessly linger. A General Manager I liked named Jean-Richard left after being promoted. When they announced his replacement, my supervisor and I ran to the phone and called The Weasel to get the 411 on the new guy.

"He's about our age," The Weasel said.

"What's he like, personality-wise?"

"He reminds me of Danny DeVito," was all The Weasel said.

"Danny DeVito? Is he short?"

"No," he said. "He just reminds me of him. Not sure why exactly."

His name was Alberto. He came in quietly enough and didn't seem like the gangbusters type. He put so much product in his black hair that I started calling him "Alberto V05." The name stuck with the other employees. If he ever caught on he didn't let me know.

Now Jean-Richard was great to work with, but he did end up having a beef with me. Annually around Thanksgiving the bank would organize an event they called the "Turkey Bowl," where they rented a bowling alley and the branches would have a day at the lanes. Jean-Richard brought his wife and family, and we were all having a good time. There were door prizes and the year before I had won a turkey. That year, Jean-Richard walked up to me during our first game and handed me a bottle of wine and a frozen turkey, saying I had won a prize. He took a picture of me holding both, so I assumed that I had won both. No one told me otherwise. I placed the turkey and the wine on the seat next to mine. As we continued to bowl I grew concerned that the bird would thaw, and feared I would forget to take the wine home with me at the end of the afternoon, so I took my prizes and put them in the trunk of my car, parked just outside the alley to keep them cool on that autumn afternoon. Jean-Richard's wife gave me the stink-eye the rest of the time I was there. I thought that perhaps I had once again, without realizing it, committed some obscure faux pas that neurotypicals deem unforgivable. I later found out that my only prize was the wine, and not the turkey, which in fact Jean-Richard had won. (My hand to the sky I thought I had won both.) Jean-Richard informed me of this months later at the bank's Christmas party, in front of my coworkers no less, practically accusing me of stealing food from his family's mouth. Why didn't anybody say anything at the alley?

Jean-Richard wisely left the customer service manager to deal with the tellers, only calling us in for our quarterly evaluation. He would look at our records, thank us for hitting our goals, say we would get our bonuses, and that was it. Meeting over in five. I had even won his praise after foiling a fraudster with a phony Government of Canada Department of Defense cheque.

One important thing to know is that there is not one job at a bank, from part-time teller to CEO, that can't be done by anyone as long as they can read, write, and count. All you need to know is easily taught. Way easier than one may think. Most branch managers I worked for did not even have an undergraduate degree. They recruited Alberto from a department store, and he worked his way up from teller. He turned out to be another over-eager busybody micro-manager.

All bank employees had sales goals based on a point system. Opening an account was, say, 50 points. A credit card was 100 points. A mortgage, the really big kahuna, was like 10,000 points or whatever. Tellers had to make 500 points a quarter to make their quota and receive their bonuses. Fair enough. Easy enough. Points were awarded for signing up customers for telephone or computer banking (a service that was intended to put us tellers out of work), or for increasing credit limits on cards, or overdraft protection. We were a good team, so at the end of the quarter if one of us came up short another would throw the business their way to ensure we all made our quotas.

Alberto had an ally and in this case it was the receptionist Julianna, a thirty-year-plus veteran of the institution who was his total stooge. He asked her to watch me and make a report on anything I did that showed character or personality. She didn't like me because the previous manager of customer service was her friend, and the new one wouldn't let her get away with bossing the tellers around and acting like she had more authority than her pay grade.

One day Julianna came into the teller area waving a piece of paper before my face in front of clients and said to me, so loudly the whole branch could hear, that I had made a serious mistake on a deposit.

"Lemme see that," I said.

I examined the slip. I was Teller number six; that was the number on my stamp, unique to me.

"Uh, Julianna," I said, "this isn't me. The date says April 6, but the teller who did this is number four."

That took the wind from her sails.

"Oh," she said, "well, what am I supposed to do with this now?"

"I can think of several things," I said.

The clients laughed.

When we had to close at the end of the day, we needed a code from the manager of customer service, the branch manager, or one of the other officers, which Julianna decidedly was not. But Alberto allowed her to do so. I'm not sure why; it was a breach of the bank's operational rules. When a teller was ready to close, they would call for a supervisor. When I was ready that day I called out: "I need a code from a respected, hard-working, qualified manager … or Julianna!" The entire staff died of laughter save for her and Alberto. They both got really steamed, but I didn't care. It was worth it.

At quarterly evaluation time Alberto called me into his office.

"Andreas," he said, leaning forward and cocking his head to one side in an overconfident and condescending way that someone who was not bright, classy or deserving of his position in humanity and was trying in vain to hide it would, "you made your goals, but then you stopped. I'm told [by Julianna, I bet] that you share sales with others so they can hit their targets."

The most frustrating part of dealing with V05 was that he didn't know how dumb he was. He probably hasn't read a book on his own in his life. Those evaluations reminded me of Henrik Ibsen's *An Enemy of the People*, a play that explores what a travesty it is when the ignorant hold authority over the learned. One of my CEGEP teachers once regaled me with a tale of the time he worked for the United Nations and a group of drunken rebels took him and his driver hostage, forcing him to bargain and beg for their lives. The moral of his story, as he put it: "There is nothing worse than having your life in the hands of stupid people."

"Well, they encourage us to work as a team, don't they? But what difference does it make? All the total sales go to the branch, right? What's the big deal? The branch hit its goals."

"But you reach your quota and stop. Why don't you continue?"

"I'm saving them to make the numbers the next quarter," I said.

"Andreas, I want you to succeed. You work hard and the customers and other tellers like you."

"So, what's the problem?" I said. "It sounds like you are reprimanding me for doing my job. And doing it well."

He became annoyed. "Well, I'm going to increase the quotas!"

"And I'll gladly make those, too," I said, knowing that regardless of the results the bank was constantly increasing the quotas in what was a cycle of unsustainability, wanting to make sure the clients borrow and borrow until they are in such heavy debt that they will have to make endless interest payments, tying them to the financial institution for life, like a boa constrictor slowly, coldly suffocating its prey. The powers that be constantly told us to work as a team, then they delight in setting us up to fight amongst ourselves for the petty scraps they deem fit to throw at us, and then label their workers ungrateful when we complain or ask for the slightest amount of dignity.

V05 was just another corporate puppet looking to move up on the backs of those he felt were beneath him. He resented that I was educated and didn't talk like a two-bit hood in a Scorsese movie.

"Okay, fine! Whatever! You get your bonus, now get out!"

I rose and left his office, proud in the knowledge that no matter what he thought, I did my job and did it well. Until I didn't.

A few months after that incident we were having a staff meeting in Alberto's office. He told us we were going to have our holiday party at a local Asian restaurant called "Hot & Spicy." Wise-ass that I am, I piped up and said, "Are you sure you want to go there? I heard the food is cold & bland."

"No," Alberto said, ignoring our laughter, "it's a good place."

Alberto, denser than a collapsing star, had to have my little quip explained to him. He stared daggers at me. A few weeks earlier, he had contacted head office and asked them to send their top customer service evaluator, Pierre B., a slim, shy, thirtysomething who hugged his clipboard as he stood, almost unnoticed, observing us. V05 was hoping Pierre B. would see how flawed I was and recommend I be disciplined or fired. (I had met Pierre B. before; most tellers had the pleasure. The times we were sent downtown to update our skills, he was the one who supervised the training.) After three days he gave Alberto his report. We didn't know the results until we had the aforementioned staff meeting and Alberto, pissed because we were laughing at him, revealed that Pierre B. said all the tellers at our branch were great, but he singled me out as the outstanding member of the team. He especially liked the way I made personal connections with customers and kept the atmosphere light and fun. Alberto ranted out loud and in no uncertain terms in front of all, as if he were the only sane one in the room, why no one else saw how awful I was at the job. When he finished, those in attendance sat in awkward silence. That was the moment he totally lost the room, except for Julianna. (What Alberto failed to grasp was that the scripts head office gave tellers to use with the customers were just a guideline for those without experience. They didn't mind if we didn't follow it exactly, as long as we performed at a high level and the customers were happy.)

V05 was just waiting for me to mess up, and I gave him exactly what he wanted. I let down my guard one day and was bamboozled by an identity thief for $1200. The boss had me dead-to-rights. That was a fireable offence, although he didn't have to fire me. It was completely at his discretion. I could just be given a written and oral reprimand, and have a black mark on my employee record. He would not have fired anyone else at the branch, especially the attractive blonde he eventually dated and married.

The Manager of Customer Service took me aside and suggested I transfer out of there because Alberto was going to do what it took to have me canned like Green Giant corn, but if I bowed out and transferred somewhere else, he would not pursue the matter further.

"They are hiring in the credit card division. It is a higher level and the pay is better. I will give you a recommendation. Go while you still can." She even helped me apply online.

I got the gig. The branch threw me a goodbye party and a number of the clients lined up to shake my hand. Some even gave me gifts. I have not been so sad to leave a workplace before or since in my life. In my last few weeks at branch I made sure I was number one in sales, just to piss V05 off, prove my worth and show him what he was losing. (What determined your ranking was the percentage you achieved over your quota. For example, a teller with a quota of 500 who sold 1000 was at 200%, while someone on the personal banking side, whose quota was decidedly higher, and it must be said, more difficult, like 5000, and who sold 7500 would attain 150%, which would score them below the aforementioned teller despite larger overall sales; at the end of the quarter I was at 300%.)

A month later I was working downtown at the Quebec head office. The credit card division was a call centre that occupied three floors of a building in Old Montreal and had about two hundred employees and managers working there. They were an odd assortment: musicians and artists; banking veterans waiting for their pensions, and students, both full and part-time; full-fledged employees looking to move up and contract workers seeking a permanent job; even a couple of former pro athletes.

What I didn't know was that I was walking into a toxic environment that was ready to explode. It took me a few weeks to catch on. People from various positions kept trying to get me on their side. From what I could piece together, the team leaders were all friends and they only promoted and gave good schedules to their buddies and compatriots, and the staff were fed up with all that bullshit. Add to that there was a rotating work schedule that had us constantly working six days in a row, and then two days off. While technically legal, it frustrated most of us. We hated it. After a few months, I began applying to other divisions. I didn't get the jobs, but I was consistently interviewed.

So we voted in a union and then the powder keg exploded. The bank started hassling the ring leaders until they all quit, and then things got worse.

They promoted an employee who started showing up in flip-flops and shorts. Dress around the office was casual, and on weekends we could wear what we wanted, but he wore this on weekdays. And he was lousy at his job. Another guy, who was put in charge of operations, gave his girlfriend the best schedule, ahead of more seasoned employees. And if she didn't like the hours, he would go around and lean on other workers to switch shifts with her.

The employees raised enough of a stink that a high-ranking executive from Toronto personally came to tell the staff, including the managers, at a meeting attended by all three floors, that the company's policy is to give promotions based on experience and merit and not because someone was getting married, or about to have a kid, or needed more money, or was friends with a certain person.

Fair enough.

The next day a promotion was given out to another chum of a manager. It was as if the bigwig had said nothing. Then again, the higher-ups at the bank didn't seem to get anything that was going on. Once a year we had to fill out anonymous questionnaires ranking our job satisfaction. 5 was the highest, and 1 the lowest. Most categories averaged 2 to 4, but the last question, "[so and so] Bank does a good job matching my pay to performance" consistently averaged 1 and the brain-dead jerks either didn't get it or more likely chose to ignore it. Want us to be happy? Pay us better. Not rocket science. Instead, they kept giving us meaningless prizes like vouchers to buy merchandise that had the corporate logo on it. Yes, our bonus was the honour of going around advertising for the company.

One of the things they did to appease us was free food. Once a month or so they would have a pizza day or chicken day. At the time I was flat broke and desperate for any break. I worked shifts that started between noon and 4 pm that paid a little more. They consistently ordered way too much and left the food in the cafeteria, completely unsupervised. On those days I would bring tin foil and plastic bags. I showed up before my shift began, ate, came back during my lunch, ate again, and then after my shift, I grabbed what I could and took it home. When we had chicken day, they delivered hundreds of boxes of individual meals that consisted of a chicken breast or leg, fries, coleslaw, a bun, and sauce. I would do my two-meal thing, then hide some boxes in the large, unused cabinets in the cafeteria, so I could eat them over the next few days. I was surprised the first time I opened one to find others had done the same thing. That evening as I was leaving, I went to get a box of chicken for home only to find one of my fellow employees, Jean-Francois, grabbing four or five boxes.

"For the weekend?" I asked.

"No," he said, "I plan to pass these out to homeless people on my way home. You taking yours home?"

"Ahh, yeah, I guess."

"*Trés bien*."

We were not given sales quotas at the call center, but management decided to try an experiment. They created a sales derby, similar to what they did at branch, based on the bank's point system, to see how we would do. I ignored the whole silly thing because we were not going to get any extra money for it…until another employee told me that I wouldn't be able to win even if I tried. It took me two weeks to pass him, and on the last day, I won the sales derby by one point. The trophy they gave me was non-engraved (cheap bastards) and each person in the top ten got the exact same one. The credit card division President sent me a congratulatory email. It made me happy. I was proud to be the champ.

Another thing they did was pay for team lunches at a restaurant. Once a quarter the team leader would take their group, between six and nine people, out to a sports bar a few streets down from the office, paid for by the bank. When the team I was on had its turn, they all ordered burgers or chicken. By coincidence I ordered last, and I asked for the 12 oz. New York cut sirloin, one of the more expensive items on the menu. The whole team, including the leader, instantly turned on me. I'm not sure if it was because they wished they had the guts to do what I did, or that they feared if head office saw the bill they would stop having the paid lunches. I liked the steak, even if my co-workers glared at me while I ingested my meal and did not speak to me for weeks after.

Sometimes in life, you have to go for it: Once The Weasel brought me to a Habs game and we had seats in a private loge. The food was hot dogs, hamburgers, fries, pizza, and smoked meat…no complaints here. Between the second and third periods, the dessert cart arrived. After I was served a slice of cake, the attendant held up two dispensers and asked: "*Chocolat ou caramel, Monsieur*?"

"*Puis-je avoir les deux, s'il vous plait*?" I asked.

"*Mais bien sûr*!" he said, as he covered my cake in both with a big smile on his jovial face.

It doesn't hurt to ask.

The bank gave us a skating day at the Bell Amphitheatre and a harbour cruise day (both with full meals) as well as a trip to La Maison Hantée, a haunted house-themed restaurant that was quite popular for a long time in Montreal, all of which I appreciated. The medical insurance was top-shelf, and they had a program where employees could buy shares in the company, which they would subsidize, and I was a happy participant in that program. And there were a number of other benefits. We just wanted a little more money, fair opportunity, and just a little more esteem and fairness; all things that could have been done quite painlessly.

To tell the truth, the shenanigans in the office with regards to promotions didn't bother me all that much, with the exception of flip-flop guy, until it happened to me.

I applied for a higher-level position and waited. And waited. But I didn't get an interview. That was not uncommon because sometimes the jobs were posted months in advance. Then I heard via the grapevine that Harry, someone who had not been with the bank for a year, used to work at Walmart, and was hired because his girlfriend worked in the credit department, got the gig. On top of that, she was best friends with the manager who decided who was getting the promotion.

The only reason they list the jobs on the company website is because they have to. I found out from The Weasel that most managers already decide on who gets the posting beforehand and the rest is a formality, all of which the bosses at head office were quite aware of but wouldn't admit. It is required by bank rules that the managers see at least a quarter of the applicants. I asked around and more than a dozen others had applied for the same job, and like me none of them were interviewed. The head office douchebag was a total fraud. It was all just talk. The game was rigged.

Eighty percent of landing a job is getting your foot in the door. I realize that I was hired because I knew someone, but I still had to pass muster. I have no problem with anyone who gets in that way to an entry level position. And yes, I am aware that I had made a few mistakes, but no more and no worse than anyone else's. I earned each promotion and second chance with the company and I believe that I, and my co-workers, a number of whom I admit were better than I was and deserved the position more than I did, merited at least a decent shot. For me it was really about the principle, and that they lied to our faces and we had to just sit and take it.

Moving up in the ranks of the bank can be complicated and political, as I'm sure it is with most large corporations. Early in my tenure The Weasel suggested I take up golf. The bank had an annual golf tournament that was the best place to meet the top brass and get noticed. He told me about a guy named Serge, a relatively young but quite dynamic executive whose job it was to scout new talent. He would carry around a small notebook and keep track of people whom he felt had potential. If he liked the cut of your jib, it would open you up to certain opportunities. If you were boorish and difficult, if you were obnoxious or otherwise stood out for the wrong reasons, you would make his book, but in the naughty section. So I went to Canadian Tire and bought a set of sticks and proper shoes, and started to attend those outings, really getting into golf culture and spending some evenings at the driving range to improve my game. I got to play at some of the most exclusive clubs in the Montreal area for free; places that would not even consider hiring a guy like me as a caddy. The first time I showed up to play, The Weasel admonished me for wearing a South Park cap. (I hadn't totally sold out.) I don't think I caught Serge's eye, for better or worse. I had fun for the most part and got to meet a few cool people despite not fitting in and finding the brown-nosing aspect of the whole thing a tad distasteful.

I started raising a fuss and writing letters to upper management. The union by then had collapsed and so I had no one to go to there. They sent my immediate supervisor, a Ricky Schroeder look-alike army veteran to talk to me. He was a square guy and a good boss; the kind one could speak with and confide in when there was a problem and who didn't talk down to you. He seldom raised his voice or threw what you told him back in your face.

I spoke with him in his cubicle and he was towing the company line. I liked him too much to call bullshit, but I reminded him of an incident.

"Remember last year when I interviewed for the job on Nun's Island?" I said. "Did I complain when I didn't get it?"

"Well, you were a little bummed, but no you didn't ..."

"You know why? Because I was given a fair interview. In my life, I've never complained about losing in a fair fight. But dude, the dice are loaded here."

He didn't argue. He knew I was right. So he arranged for me to get a regular 10-6 Monday to Friday schedule and even put me as a trainer and occasional resource officer, which I appreciated. It meant that the bank at least respected my efforts.

But I still complained, to anyone who would listen, and a few who wouldn't. Harry, the smarmy little Greek shit who was getting the promotion, short and pudgy, who smoked like a chimney, had thinning, blonde hair, and wore thick glasses (he was not unlike Paul Williams sans the song writing talent and likeability), waddled up to me in the hallway and whispered in my ear: "Hey, Andreas. Another position is opening up in six months, *rhé*." He wanted me to pipe down and not ruin it for him. What a dick.

I was so disgusted I just walked away.

Annie, the manager behind the promotion, finally called me into her office. She gave me the same song and dance, but I wasn't having it. She was yet another person who thought she was smarter than she actually was.

I called her out on her friendship with Harry's girlfriend, which caught her off guard; she was unaware of the intelligence I had on her.

"Look," I said, "I know the score. You want me to back off? Sure. You haven't yet made the official announcement, have you? Just give all who applied a fair interview. If you still think Harry's more deserving, I will shut up. What do you say?"

She looked at me in disbelief.

"I'm not doing that, Andreas," she said. "Who told you that Harry got the promotion?"

It was at that moment I realized she just wanted me to give her the name of the person who spilled the beans on the whole matter, something I will not do to this day, even though at this point it was almost twenty years ago and that person no longer works there.

"I guess we have nothing more to talk about," I said as I rose and walked out of her office, without being dismissed.

The Weasel by then had become a financial adviser and worked at another bank. He told me that they were in the process of renovating and restructuring the head office and were looking for staffers; he could get me a shot at some of the open positions. After three tough and thorough interviews I was offered a job as assistant to the office manager and soon gave my notice to the old place, but because I was going to work for the competition they let me go with pay right away. I sent a goodbye memo to all in the office, pompously quoting the song "My Way" and ending with a line I borrowed from Letterman's goodbye address to NBC: "… not once have I been anything less than 100% proud of my association with [the bank] and I can only hope in some small way that [the bank] took a little pride in some of the things I did on their behalf."

On my last day Annie came up to me.a said that I was a good employee. I thanked her for her kind words and shook her hand. Then I got the hell out of there.

The new place was quite different from a credit card call center. It was an investment office. High-pressure. High finance. No-nonsense investment professionals playing with huge amounts of money. People were stiff and for the most part humourless. Not a good fit for this guy.

I started to learn the job and made some allies, but there were those that didn't get me; like, *really* didn't get me. Being the new guy I made mistakes, mostly small ones due to my inexperience, and soon the place was split into pro and anti-Andreas factions. I was oblivious to who my real enemies were and failed to watch my step and be careful with my smart mouth, inadvertently offending some people. Complaints were piling up with my boss, of which I was unaware.

My main job was to reset the office, have desks moved, and set up computers and phones after a massive renovation.

We had ordered and received a new fax machine. When it arrived I installed it right away. Then my supervisor called me into her office.

"Who told you to set it up?" she asked.

"No one. I thought it was my job to take care of the office and ..."

"Well," she said, "you were supposed to let someone from the manufacturer come in for that!"

"I didn't know. Nobody told ..."

"Do you still have the box it came in?"

"I threw it away."

"What!?! Go get it! Now!"

She instructed me to put it back the way I found it and call the company to send a technician. So I dug the box out of the recycling and put it back the way it was delivered. I even taped the box shut; the perfect crime.

Why was she so angry? When the technician arrived it took her twenty minutes to set it up the exact same way I did.

Now one must understand the office was made up of financial advisors who were partners with the bank, but it was their own little businesses, and on occasion another bank would poach them with a better offer and they would defect with their clients and portfolio. That happened once on my watch.

I showed up to work to find that an F.A. with a huge list of wealthy clients had cleared out his files during the night and bolted to another bank. I was not yet briefed on the proper procedure for such matters. There was a furious panic. I asked my boss what to do, and she said, "Cancel his phone, cancel his computer access!" Which I immediately did. Then later in the day the *Capo di tutti Capi* of the Quebec office came in and announced he was able to top the competition's offer and the F.A. was coming back.

Why would they want such a disloyal, fickle jerk back in the fold? I thought.

I was told to reinstate his phone and computer access, which are invaluable to a stock trader. The market could change in an instant and they need a quick reaction. Otherwise their clients could go broke in a day. But I had cancelled them and it would take days to set the services up again.

The *Capo* yelled in my face in front of the whole office: "Why did you do that? You were only supposed to put it on hold!"

"I've only been here a few months. No one told me that," I said, waiting for my boss to pipe up and take responsibility, which didn't happen. Feeling betrayed as I looked at her and she remained silent, and not knowing what else to do, I broke down. Pointing at my boss I said, "She said to cancel it. They heard her. Ask them. They all heard her. No one told me just to put it on hold. I had no idea you could do that."

In hindsight, I should have just apologized and taken the rap. My instinct was totally wrong. If I had absorbed the blame, being new I might have been forgiven and gained an important ally in the office manager.

The next day I could not find the blue buggy I used to cart around heavy boxes. I sent out an office-wide memo asking if anyone had seen it. Someone replied that it was in the 14th-floor closet, and the defector had used it to return his client files to his new, much larger office. Some asshole must have complained because the Sub-Capo, a slim and slickly dressed up-and-comer, emailed me and told me not to bother the staff with trivial matters like that. I went to his office explaining that the equipment was my responsibility and that it would cost over $300 to replace it. My memo led to it being recovered. What was the problem? I guess he didn't like to be confronted, especially with logic.

The following week I completed the reorganization of the office on a Friday. That Monday I showed up ready for my final task: calling a company to haul away over fifty boxes of records. I came in, turned my computer on, and sat at my desk. My boss called me into the conference room. When I arrived she was sitting there with Jean-André, the head commandant of the floor above ours. He was a large, fat, sloppy man who looked like a pig with glasses; so much so that I think I once saw him floating above a Pink Floyd concert. He didn't say a word. My boss asked me to sit down. She told me that my services were no longer required and I would receive two weeks' salary. Then she gave me a taxi coupon to go home and informed me that I had fifteen minutes to gather my stuff and hit the bricks.

I calmly stood up, took the coupon, and went to my desk. I cleared out my things and walked to the elevator with Jean-André oinking right behind me. No one in the office looked at me as I left, except for one broker who exited his office and bravely shook my hand and wished me well, adding he was sorry to see me go. The Swine and I got into the elevator and did not exchange a word. When I got out on the ground floor he said "Good luck" and I whispered a "fuck you" so low that he probably didn't hear. I wanted to turn around and direct him to the bacon factory, but if I did he could screw with my severance pay and vital unemployment paperwork.

So … where do I go from here? I asked myself.

Home, I guess.

"Taxi!"

* * *

The next day I secured a Thursday morning appointment with a head hunter who specialized in financial services.

I went to a barber for a haircut and a shave the day before. I had my blue, double-breasted suit pressed. I shined my best shoes. I was ready.

My dad gave me a lift to the interview. When I arrived the place took me by surprise. I was expecting an elaborate office. Instead, I found a bare-bones operation. All the employees were in casual dress. With my attire and briefcase I looked like a corporate honcho from head office who had come by to check out the place.

The guy I had the appointment with was dressed in a polo shirt and khakis. He insisted I call him by his first name and he led me to his cubicle and offered me a seat. Then he asked me to tell him about myself. I told him about my education and employment history as he leaned back in his chair, listening to me intently. When I was done I said, "So, can you help me find a new job?"

"No."

After an awkward pause, I said, "No?"

"No. You are all wrong for banking. You should be in show business or something."

"What?"

"Look, I've been doing this a long time," he said, despite the fact that his entire operation looked like it sprouted up overnight. (I found out later that he was not an employee, but the owner of the firm.) "You are not right for financial services. Not at all the type."

"But I've been doing it for over seven years. I need a job."

"From what you told me, you'll probably get unemployment insurance, right? You plan to apply?"

"Yeah."

"Tell you what: If you get the U.I., take the summer off. Think about what you want to do. If by September you still want a job in banking, I'll see what I can get you. But you are not a match for this kind of work. Trust me."

I thanked him and left quite confused.

I sold the shares I had accumulated from my old bank over the seven years I had worked there. It was enough to get me out of debt and then some. And I got the U.I. so I heeded his advice and decided to take full advantage of my first summer off since University.

Most of my classmates upon graduation took long trips abroad to find themselves. My family did not have upper-middle class money so I couldn't do that. But now I had the time and some money, so why not finally do it myself? But if I left Canada I would lose my unemployment benefits, and I had to look for work. So I signed up with some employment agencies, and planned to travel across the country in between occasional interviews.

In late July I took a road trip to Toronto to see some old friends. Then I continued on to Burlington to see my college buddy Rick, who was nice enough to invite me to stay with his family. His wife set me up with one of her friends, a singing paralegal, and I ended up spending half the summer living with her in Mississauga. I did some job hunting while in the GTA, but nothing came of it. Our romance ended on the last day of summer and I went home.

But what to do? Should I dive fully into looking for work now? What was I meant to do?

I had been writing a blog since 2003 so I decided to make it into a full-fledged website with podcasts. Another college buddy, Phil, told me where to download software and pod-safe music to create such fare, and I started recording and editing. I had not had so much fun since my time at CFCD, Dawson College Television.

I came to realize that I should be working in a field that was more for me. Money was not important. All those years I didn't fully launch myself into the world was because I wasn't happy. Until that point, throughout my working life, with the exception of a happy few months at one of the branches, I was constantly on the verge of quitting my job and running home and hiding under my bed, tired of the world and its difficulties. I had to find what I was meant to do.

When January rolled around I started to seriously seek a career job. So I did what didn't work last time: I printed a stack of CVs and went in search of gainful employment. It was unseasonably warm that year. I put on a nice shirt and tie and was off. I started at the Atwater Metro and walked up Ste. Catherine Street, visiting any and all record stores, book stores, TV stations, radio stations, and newspapers I could find. I went to buildings and scanned the directories. Any production companies? Communications companies? Anything that looked interesting to me. If so I would leave them a CV, but most places gave them right back and told me to apply online at their website. I had not looked for work like that in years, and the times had changed without me noticing.

At the end of the day, I went online to apply for jobs, including employment websites, and signed up for anything I could find that was more *me*. I got nothing. No replies. Not even a Thank You for applying. Those employment websites are all bullshit. They make you fill out an online questionnaire, write a cover letter and jump through various other hoops and then nothing happens. Then they try to sell you their "premium membership," which I guess means you pay for nothing to happen. I don't know one person who found their dream job, or any decent job, that way. Just about all my jobs were the result of knowing someone. Those websites are not places where dreams come true, unless you are the sleazy businessperson who owns it and revels in finding desperate people to exploit with low-paying, crappy gigs.

I soon was interviewed for a management job at a large chain bookstore. I thought I did well, but I didn't get a callback. When I finally lost my patience and contacted them, the store's director, who annoyingly said my name with a Greek accent, told me that head office made him give the position to someone with better connections. (In fairness, they were more experienced.)

As time went by I was starting to get desperate for anything. I would look at online ads and apply for office assistant jobs or whatever I could find and the next day my phone would ring for the pre-interviews. Most of the time I didn't get past that, but when I did and I showed up they'd all say the same thing: I was over-qualified.

I felt like saying, "No I'm not! I totally suck! Hire me!"

I even had an interview at a small bookstore in a Dorval shopping mall for a full-time position. The ad said that it paid more than minimum wage. Turns out it was 25¢ more. The manager, a late middle-aged hippie, saw me and immediately said she wasn't going to take me on. I was too old and overqualified. We ended up talking for over an hour about other things, but again I left with nothing to show for my efforts.

My U.I. was expiring soon, so I got desperate. I looked for jobs with insurance companies. I received a phone call from one of them. I didn't want to work for another bank, let alone an insurance company, but my back was to the wall.

"Well," the interviewer said, "you would have to take a course on insurance."

"Okay," I said, getting shaky.

"And the course is in French. Can you do that?"

"*Aucun problème.*"

"And you have to …"

"Wait!" I said, coming to my senses. "No! I can't do any of this. Sorry!" And hung up the phone.

What am I doing? How did I get here?

I found prospective employment with an investment firm on the West Island. They were looking for an office assistant and called me to come in for an interview. At the time I had one week of U.I. left. I knew I had to make this work. Another haircut and shave, another pressing for my suit. I spent two days psyching myself up, getting my confidence going. Repeating to myself, "They are going to like me. I am going to get this job."

I was told to be there after 4 pm. Fair enough. The market closed at 4 pm and I guess the guy doing the interviewing wanted to watch the trends.

I arrived on time. The investment company was in a building along the highway that looked like a pyramid made of gold. I was politely brought straight to the office of the boss. He was a man who looked in his mid-forties, impeccably dressed in a three-piece suit and jet-black, gelled-back hair. He greeted me warmly and asked where I was from.

"Park Ex," I said. It turns out he grew up there as well.

So far, so good.

He asked me to tell him about myself. I gave him the greatest pitch of my life. My personality and confidence filled the room. I struggled to keep eye contact and stay focused and on message, but I was smashing it. I was twelve feet tall. I was bulletproof.

When I finished he looked at me and said, "Wow. That was amazing."

"Thank you," was all I could think to say.

"Why aren't you president of a company?" he said with a smile. I was not sure if he was being sarcastic or not. I froze. But I had to say something.

"So, do I get the job?" I asked.

"What job?"

"The office manager job? The one you posted on the website?"

"Oh, that! No. You're not what I'm looking for. I want a forty-five year-old five-foot-two white English-speaking woman for that job. Someone the clients here on the West Island would identify with. Even so, the job doesn't start until September."

September was months away.

"So, why am I here?" I said, afraid of the answer.

"We want to know about Theo."

"Who?"

"Theo. Y'know, Theodore X."

"I don't know who that is."

"You don't?"

"No. Why? Should I? Who is that?"

He explained it to me: It turns out Theo was his business partner who one day up and defected to another company with the bulk of their portfolio. He figured since I was Greek I must have known him and he just wanted to know what Theo was up to and why he did that. I told him I didn't know who Theodore X was and had no idea any of that had transpired.

"All right then," he said. "Thank you for coming in."

He shook my hand and I left, dumbfounded.

What kind of person plays a game with someone's life like that? One week left on my U.I.

I walked to my car like a zombie. I sat there, feeling numb. What was I going to do? I thought about driving into a cement wall, but then I noticed I had an airbag, so I might not be killed, and I didn't want to only get maimed. I thought about driving off a bridge, but could not recall one with weak guardrails. Stupid safety inspectors. I wanted to get into a serious accident, but that might hurt some innocent person and I didn't want to go out that way.

How did I get here?

By the time I snapped out of my funk, I realized that more than two hours had passed, the parking lot was empty, and the sun had set. I went to a Wendy's and got some drive thru, including the chili and cheese nachos I like so much.

A few days later I received a call. Someone I went to high school with (I guess that place wasn't a total waste), who was now Director of a renowned downtown book store, called and asked if I was still looking for work. When I said yes he asked me to come in for an interview. I thought he was going to offer me a part-time pity job until I got back on my feet, but instead he offered me a management position. During the interview when he asked if I thought I could handle the responsibilities, I literally said: “Fuck, yeah!”

He hired me anyway. The day after I received a call from the book store manager in Dorval, who told me the person she hired wasn’t working out, and the job was mine if I was available.

So good to be wanted.

ME, MOM & TRUDEAU

In the spring of 2008 The Weasel invited me to a hockey game. I'd been out of work just short of a year and the frustration of job hunting was starting to get to me. He had excellent seats in the red section, not too far up from centre ice. Although The Weasel had a number of connections for Habs tickets, he didn't use them himself all the time. Sometimes he resold them for a profit; other times he gave them away to relatives or clients as gifts.

We were on our way to our seats when I spotted out of the corner of my eye the then-aspiring politician Justin Trudeau. At the time he was unelected and had recently announced his intention to run as a candidate for the Liberal Party in the federal riding of Papineau, which included Park Extension. I was still living there then, so I decided to see if I could meet him.

There was a gentleman with him who appeared to be a handler, an assistant, or maybe even a Kingmaker. I was not sure of his role, but I knew I had to get through him to get to Trudeau. I walked up to The Handler and introduced myself.

"Hello," I said, "my name is Andreas Kessaris and I live in Park Extension ..."

I could tell he was no fool. The Handler snapped into action and knew exactly what I wanted. He wasted no time introducing me to Trudeau, who shook my hand. We spoke for a few seconds and he expressed his hope that I would support his bid for public office. The Handler then gave me his card and wished me a good evening. Overall I was satisfied with the encounter. And I got a kick out of the fact that we had better seats than they did. I met Justin Trudeau a few more times before he became Prime Minister, mostly in relation to my job as a bookstore Events Coordinator, and have worked with his mother Margaret Trudeau, and his brother Alexandre a number of times when promoting their books. (Oddly enough at the aforementioned hockey game, sitting about halfway between us and the ice was former U.S. Vice President Al Gore. I didn't get a chance to shake his hand, though. There was a hulking, no-nonsense, armed Secret Service bodyguard who looked like two men soldered together protecting him.)

I emailed The Handler, whose surname was similar to one of my favourite University professors, and asked if they were related. It turned out they were not, but he asked me to sign up for Trudeau's email list, and I said "sure thing."

By that summer I had found employment. Not long after, I received an email from the Trudeau camp inviting me to the opening of his election headquarters and the official launch of his campaign. It was on St. Denis Street, slightly north of Jean-Talon. I decided to pass by there that night on my way home from work to see what was going on. What I found was an ugly scene.

While Papineau riding includes Park Ex and Villeray, areas with large ethnic populations that tend to support the Liberal Party of Canada, it also includes heavily Francophone neighbourhoods. Some of those residents passionately and angrily remember the elder Trudeau's tireless opposition to Quebec sovereignty and over-reactive use of the War Measures Act during the October Crisis, despite the fact that most of those protesting were not yet born at the time.

There wasn't much of a police presence on hand when I arrived; it felt like a riot would break out any second. On one side were the Trudeau supporters waving Canadian flags, standing nose-to-nose with loud, obnoxious *souvranistas* holding placards with slogans that referred to Justin Trudeau as "*Le fils de PET*" and other tasteless fare. One of them was wearing a gorilla mask, the symbolism behind which eluded me. Leading the mob of mostly teenage thugs was a much older, diminutive, renowned rabble-rouser who made a name for himself with the FLQ during the October Crisis. At first, I did not see him because he was standing behind a fire hydrant. But then he moved and I saw him with his smug, self-satisfied, hateful grin, acting like he was accomplishing something.

Eventually, more police arrived and they separated the two sides. I didn't join the fray but rather observed from the sidelines. The scene remained loud and chaotic throughout my stay. There were at least a half-dozen TV news cameras there, as well as numerous other journalists from radio and print. I ran into someone I knew who was a political writer and columnist for *The Montreal Gazette*. We spoke for a bit and then I asked him what he thought about the scene unfolding before us. He smiled, shrugged, and then leaned over and said into my ear, "This can only *help* Trudeau."

I stayed until the party started inside the storefront campaign office; I could easily see what was transpiring through the large window. They had a stage set up with a lectern and a microphone. I saw The Handler in the office running things. He got up on stage and introduced Trudeau, who came out with his wife and young son, a couple of people I didn't recognize, local municipal politician Mary Deros, and my mom.

Mom!?! How the hell did she get there!?! I thought.

She stood behind the candidate for Papineau throughout his short speech. At that point I went home, shaking my head. I did not consider staying and making sure Mom got out of there safely. I would be more concerned for any *souvrainista* that had the misfortune of getting in *her* way.

Why was I surprised? That woman usually finds a way. Years later when my mother's older sister died, Mom was in the middle of a chemotherapy cycle, and was too weak to attend the viewing and funeral. I went to the viewing and apologized to my aunts, uncles, and cousins on her behalf for her absence, all of whom were fully understanding. The next day I could not attend the service because I had to work. And Mom? She was her ever-resourceful self. She got dressed, and took her walker, which can easily convert to a wheelchair, downstairs to the lobby. Her seniors' residence was five blocks from the small brown church on St. Roch. On the street she met a young lady and asked her if she could push her the rest of the way. The young lady agreed, and would not accept money for her efforts. Mom's brother-in-law gave her a ride home when it was over.

Of course she was at the launch. My mom was a fanatic for Pierre Elliot Trudeau. She became a Canadian citizen around the time he was Prime Minister and was totally swept up in Trudeaumania. She has proudly proclaimed that the first time she voted in Canada, it was for him.

To my mom, Pierre Trudeau was the epitome of class and sophistication and could do no wrong. When she tried to get me to do things like shave daily or iron my shirts properly or keep my hair neat, especially when I worked in banking, she would say: "*Eftôh khanee* ôh *Pierre Trudeau*" (That's what Pierre Trudeau does).

The next day I asked her if she was invited on stage and no surprise she was not. She told me she went to the party with friends from her seniors' group, talked her way inside, and slowly moved closer to the stage. Fortunately for all involved, she was not an assassin. Mom knew no one would try to stop a woman in her seventies so she just decided to go for it. Then she related to me the story of how she met the elder Trudeau, something of which I was completely unaware.

When Pierre Elliot Trudeau left politics in the early 80s he bought an art deco house called Maison Ernest-Cormier on Pine Avenue in Montreal and it was no secret. Everyone knew where he lived. He worked at a law office downtown and was known to walk to and from there daily with no protection from the RCMP.

So Mom decided one day in the mid-90s that she wanted to meet Pierre Trudeau. She put on her finest clothes, made herself up, and on a sunny autumn day took the 80 bus downtown and walked up Pine Avenue until she arrived at 1418. Then she rang the doorbell.

According to Mom, Trudeau's housekeeper soon answered the door.

"Yes?" she said, "Can I help you?"

"I want to meet Mr. Trudeau," Mom said.

The Housekeeper stood silent for a moment.

"Please," Mom said.

Another moment went by and The Housekeeper said: "Just a second," and closed the heavy wooden door.

After about two minutes the door opened again. Standing there in a leisure suit and sandals was the former prime minister.

"Yes," he said, "what can I do for you?"

Mom wouldn't tell me what they talked about; maybe she doesn't remember, maybe she just wants to keep that for herself. She will probably take that secret with her to the grave. She only said he was pleasant, friendly, polite, and a total gentleman...exactly what she thought he would be, and that he patiently and politely stayed until she ended the conversation by thanking him for his time.

Then, after a moment of reflection, she added that he was a lot smaller and skinnier in person than she thought he would be.

THE AMBUSH

Introducing my girlfriends to my parents was, for me, a constant source of stress. Mom and Dad's English was suspect and French was practically non-existent. For the most part, I have not dated Greeks, much to their chagrin. Add my mom being Supreme Master of the Butt-inskis to Dad and his crude, crass, and I have to say, sexist sense of humour, and we have a formula for a nightmarish encounter. It was quite the juggling act, to say the least. Living with Mom for as long as I did, run-ins with my girlfriends were unavoidable, but for the most part, she made a good effort … until Lana.

I don't know if it was because that relationship came right after I broke up with Mel, who my mom adored, or if she just didn't like her, but Lana was an instant target of Mom's scorn. Lana and I were together for two years, and while it wasn't something to do with Mom that ultimately led to the end of the relationship, it certainly didn't help. After that was over, I did the best I could to keep anyone I was seeing away from her.

It became easier after I moved out, and while my girlfriends were wonderful people, I promised myself that unless it was really, heavily serious, I would not bring them home to Mother, not that any were particularly kinky girls, as the song sort of goes. Then, I met Kay.

We had known each other casually for years, while we were both seeing other people, but when the relationship began we hit it off so well that I knew it was not long before she and Mom would meet.

Mom lives in a seniors' residence and has been fighting multiple myeloma, a form of blood cancer, for years. Because her illness weakened her bones, she could not get a much-needed hip replacement surgery and she can only move about with the aid of a walker. At that time, COVID-19 lockdown was in effect so Kay and I couldn't go up to her apartment, and spring was taking its sweet time to arrive, making it too cold to meet outside. The only place we could get together was the small lobby of her residence for a masked, distanced visit. Mom was to greet us there at the agreed time.

If there were a meter that measured anxiety, mine would have been in the high red. I didn't know what to expect from my unpredictable and opinionated mother. In the past she would say to me "*eftie, m'aresi*" (I like her) or "*eftie, then m'aresi*" (I don't like her). She said that as though how she felt about them would make a difference to me. Of course, it didn't. All that meant to me was that Mom would make the relationship easy or a hemorrhoid, but it didn't change anything else in the least.

When we arrived on that cold, damp, dark afternoon, Mom was already in the lobby, sitting on her large, elaborate walker. She greeted us warmly and then gave Kay the once-over with her eyes. We stood before my white-haired mother as she sat in her seat, raising her chin high like a Queen holding court.

The conversation was friendly. She asked Kay what she did for a living. Kay tried to explain that she was a graduate student who taught part-time. My mother was not up on academics and looked confused.

"What do you teach?" Mom said.

"Poetry and composition. Writing, mostly."

"What *eez* that? How do you do that?" Mom said, not clear on the terminology.

"Well, I teach workshops where I get the students to reflect on their life experiences, and write about themselves ..."

"Like a psychologist!" Mom said.

Kay looked at me. I shrugged.

"Ah, yeah," Kay said, "like a psychologist."

A few more minutes of polite conversation ensued, then Mom reached into the storage compartment at the bottom of her walker and pulled out a clear plastic bag. In it were her treasured string of pearls and matching earrings, the last of her expensive and valued jewellery collection that she had not sold off or given away.

"Okay, I called *thee tsertst*; they have time for a wedding on Wednesday. You two are going to get married, and you," she said as she pointed at Kay, "are going to wear *theese* pearls."

Kay and I looked at each other. Neither of us had expected that. I guess Mom did like her. I knew why she was doing this: She was eighty-six at the time and sick. She had lived long enough to be a grandmother, and now simply wanted to see one of her children get married. Still, I thought she was going a little off the deep end.

I broke the silence.

"Mom, we are not doing that. Put your jewellery back. We have only been together a few months. And if we get married it will *not* be in the Greek Church, or any church for that matter."

"Shh! *Leesen*! *Djust* get married. I have *reeserved thee tserts*!"

Mom became more determined as I tried to explain things to her without losing my temper, to no avail. So I quickly said goodbye and hustled Kay out. I was scared to death Kay would get spooked and dump me immediately after we left.

We talked about what happened on the ride home and Kay was understanding; she even started laughing. I told her she didn't have to do anything Mom said, and after the initial shock wore off it became a bit of an inside joke between us.

Mom is not a person you fool with. Her acerbic wit is legendary. Weekdays someone from the CLSC across from her residence comes by to make her breakfast and once a week cleans and does her laundry. The aid worker once looked in Mom's refrigerator and asked, "Where is the milk?"

Mom's reply was: "There's a cow on the balcony. Go milk it."

On an occasion when I took her to Jean-Talon Market, she went up to a vendor to buy a crate of eggs.

"Are these eggs fresh?" she said.

"*Oui, madame. Dey* just come out of *da* chicken *dis* morning," the vendor said.

"Yes," Mom said, "I'm sure you were there watching."

Over time COVID restrictions slowly lifted and we started meeting Mom on a bench outside her residence. The conversations went well and Mom, when she turned on the charm and displayed her sharp sense of humour, was easier to deal with. It came to the point that, when we'd visit, Mom would ignore me and go straight to Kay to deliver a warm hug, hardly speaking to me. When I would visit her without Kay, the first thing out of her mouth was, "*pou einai ei Kay*?" (Where is Kay?). Mom had even taken to calling Kay "*thee* Golden Girl."

They were talking one time and Mom said, "Andreas, he was smart as a boy!"

"Yes," Kay said, "he's really intelligent and knows a lot of things."

Mom turned to her and said back, with serious pride: "I know what I have."

We started going on short walks along Jean-Talon Street and they would often stop at boutiques and window-shop clothing. One of the stores had a lovely, long white skirt for sale, hanging in the doorway. Mom and Kay looked it over and discussed how nice it was.

When we went home Kay said that perhaps we should buy the skirt for Mom.

"She wasn't really that interested in the skirt," I said to Kay. "She just wants to talk about clothes with another girl. She didn't have a daughter to talk to about stuff like that before."

Over a year later we came by on a Saturday afternoon, and Mom was extra excited that Kay was with me. Mom made us sit at the small dining table in her kitchen and asked us to wait there. She went into her bathroom and came out with her hands full of assorted makeup products.

* * *

Mom adores her makeup and does not leave the house without applying it, doing her hair, and otherwise looking her best, even when she goes to the hospital for her chemotherapy. When I asked why she made such an effort, her reply was, "I am still a *woo-man*! All *thee* doctor and nurse, they all say how good I *louk*!" as if she were trying to win the Ms. Cancer Ward Pageant.

My mother, like a lot of women, is fiercely loyal to her cosmetic brands and specific products. When she became ill she often dispatched me to buy her makeup, same as when I was young and she would send me out to purchase her hair dye. I had to get colour #114, and no other. When the Martel Pharmacy on St. Roch Street was out, I had to walk all the way to Jean-Talon to find the correct one.

Besides being horrified at how expensive all those products are (a small jar of night cream was $80), I was shocked at the variety. I would go to the pharmacy and walk around looking totally lost. Once I had other women in the aisle help me. They were a little older and when I explained I was buying it for my mother, who was in a seniors' residence, they took the time to help me, saying I was a "good son."

Another time she sent me with an empty container and compact, with strict instructions that I was to give them to the girl at the makeup counter, who would take it from there. I showed up at the pharmacy clutching the tiny jar, feeling like a five-year-old with a note pinned to his shirt. The sales clerk led me to the endless, intimidating makeup aisle and we began our search.

"Is that it?" I said, pointing to a box that looked exactly like what we were looking for.

"No," the makeup girl said, "that is day cream. Your mom wants night cream."

"Is there a difference?"

I believe that, when a woman looks at a man, she sees a pig, a dog, or an ape. The makeup girl eyed me at that moment like I was a chimpanzee in a varsity jacket, not even bothering to answer because I simply did not have the cranial capacity to comprehend.

After procuring the correct cream, I gave her an empty compact.

"Do you have this?" I said.

She opened it. "It's empty," she said. "I'd have to see it to know the correct shade."

"It's for my mother. She has the same skin I do."

The makeup girl looked me over for a second, then quickly handed me the product.

"This is the one," she said, with no uncertainty.

I was nervous about bringing it home. It was expensive and once opened, could not be returned. As if all women had a psychic connection, it was exactly what Mom wanted.

* * *

Back at the kitchen table, Mom laid out all her products and applicators and began to lecture Kay on how to apply makeup. Kay, who is a Gen-Xer, is quite adept at applying product when she chooses, and did not need such a lesson. At least I didn't think so. But Mom continued and we sat there quietly listening.

I don't know if she did it because she had always wanted a daughter to whom to pass on her accumulated wisdom on all things *woo-manly*, or if she wanted Kay, who is Northern European with blonde hair, blue eyes, and light skin, all traits Greeks view as recessive and thus inferior, to hide her heritage and darken up.

Mom believes a pale complexion is a sign that one is sickly and weak. When we were kids, she would make my brother and I tan during the summer "*na kanete chroma*" (to get colour), without considering the possibility of skin cancer.

I had not seen Mom so enthusiastic in such a long time. It was as if she were an Avon rep giving a demonstration. She said that I knew the products (I didn't, really) and that I would purchase them for Kay. In the middle of applying them to herself, Mom waved her hands emphatically in front of her own face and said, "You see? Bright, bright!"

Then Mom went back to her bathroom to get hair products. I whispered in Kay's ear reassuring her: "Look, you don't have to do any of this. She only wants to impart something to another girl. That's all."

Mom returned with mousse and gel, ready for the second part of the lesson.

Mom sprayed an egg-sized amount of mousse in her palm and began to work it in, saying, "*Thees* will make your hair curly…and double. Double!"

Greek women view fine, silky hair as a lesser trait. Real women have hair higher and thicker than a motorcycle helmet.

"Dina," Kay said politely, "thank you, but I don't have curly hair."

Mom stopped and shot her a serious glare.

"You *do* have curly hair! You have to *work* for *eet*!" she said, pointing a finger in Kay's face.

When the show was finally over, Mom, exhausted but satisfied, sat down and once again pulled out the clear plastic bag with the pearls.

"When I first saw you two," she said, "I knew you were one. That you will be together always. Now, will you take *thee* pearls, please? I want you to have them."

Kay looked at me. I shrugged.

"Yes," Kay said, accepting them, "thank you, Dina. I will."

By the time we reached the lobby, our shared silence had turned into fits of hysterical laughter. The true lesson of the day? With Dina, the next ambush is just around the corner.

THE NEW GURUS

My favourite summertime activity is bike riding. The second the snow is gone I tune up my wheels and enjoy Montreal's countless bicycle paths when the weather cooperates.

When riding I wear a pair of mesh gloves that leave rather unique and peculiar spotted tan lines on my hands. At work my clients are often curious as to their origin, and after I explain they seem surprised because most cyclists are slim and small and I am, to say the least, not. (That's the reason why most people say I appear to ride in slow motion.)

One day when I still worked at a bank, one of our clients, Mr. Topper, a short, late-middle-aged man, noticed my hands and asked: "Is that from golf?"

"No," I said, "from cycling."

"How long you cycle?"

"Since I was a kid."

"No!" Mr. Topper said, as though it were my fault his question was ambiguous. "How long do you ride each time you go out?"

I found it odd that he was interested in how long my treks were rather than how far or where I went, or what kind of bike I rode.

"Two or three hours, depending on the weather … sometimes longer, sometimes less."

"Oh," he said, as though my answer offended him. "So, you're not a serious rider, are you? When I go out I ride for six or more hours. I guess for you it is just a recreational activity."

"I guess so."

What is this guy's problem? I thought at the time.

I guess if I had told him that the tan marks were from golf he would inquire what my handicap was, and no matter my reply he would claim that his was better and that he could out-drive Tiger Woods. It is easy to talk down to a person when you are their client and the playing field is slanted heavily in your favour. I'm sure if we ran into each other on the street as strangers his attitude would've been quite different.

But why was it so important to him that he outdo me?

* * *

For some time people have been moving away from organized religion, disenchanted with its corruption and hypocrisy. To fill the void, a wave of New Gurus have appeared, and proven themselves to be just as corrupt and hypocritical.

A few years ago, someone I know who works in TV and film posted on their social media a series of "commandments" copied from another person's page that reflected their philosophy on life and career. He's the kind of verbose guy who, if you were to ask him if he had the time, he would tell you the story of how his watch was made; so insecure about his intelligence that he was constantly trying to prove how smart he was; the type who would write a condescending two-hundred word essay in reaction to a facetious Facebook post, totally not getting the joke, and pretentiously end it with: "Be well."

Reading it made me cringe. In essence, it said:

1. Don't ever take no crap from nobody
2. Everyone else is your pawn
3. Step over anyone to get what you want
4. Nobody is as smart as you
5. Never admit you are wrong about anything
6. Be a good person
7. Ethics are for losers
8. Go after what you want even if you are unqualified and undeserving
9. Desire alone is enough
10. The ends always justify the means

I was flabbergasted. What shocked me the most was that hidden in the middle of all that gobbledygook was a token crumb of morality.

To me, the list read like this:

1. Be a jerk
2. Be a big jerk
3. Be an even bigger jerk
4. Be an asshole
5. Be a fucking asshole
6. Be a good person
7. Be a different kind of a jerk
8. Be a dick
9. Be a total dick
10. Be a colossal dick

In response to this, I posted two things in his comments section that reflect my personal beliefs and philosophies on life and career. One is a quote attributed to Charles Bukowski where he laments about how idiots have all the confidence and intelligent people are the ones who question themselves. (To me, overconfidence is the unmistakable calling card of mediocre talent.) The other is a line Steve Martin said while being interviewed on PBS. Mr. Martin was promoting his latest book, the excellent *Born Standing Up* (which I recommend not only to those wanting to get into the arts and entertainment field, but to anyone wanting to improve themselves. It chronicles how hard he had to work to get to where he is, offering lessons that could apply to anyone aspiring to get into a professional field), and was asked what advice he had for those who were seeking a career in show business. His reply was that one should be so good that one can't be ignored.

I signed my post with "Be well." That ought to show him.

Another go-getter I knew one time reposted a similar naïve and inaccurate list of the differences between "successful" and "unsuccessful" people. For example, it said "successful" people are pleasant, do not hold grudges, and are avid readers, while "unsuccessful" people are the opposite. I don't know what ignorant fool originally wrote that claptrap but if their definition of a "successful" person is someone who has a lot of money earned in business, then they are dead wrong. If that's the case, each "successful" person I know in real life is bitter, vindictive and barely literate. The list went on to say that "successful" people lift others up, while "unsuccessful" people put others down. If the previous definition of a "successful" person applies, they are to me the ones who relish walking all over anyone when they can get away with it, and are envious of all who are happy, have real friends, true popularity, and feel good about themselves.

A few years ago there was a news story about a group of people who were attending a motivational camp. One of the activities was to hike up a mountain without water. One of the attendees died along the way while the person running the exercise, who likely had no real training in anything but being a total jerkoff, refused to give him water that he held right before him. Imagine some idiot is yelling at you and calling you weak or a loser because you could not complete a gruelling task, and that indignant bullshit is the last thing your ears hear as your life ends.

One such New Guru is a spray-tanned, cap-toothed, freaky giant whose infomercials used to play on late-night TV after *Family Ties* reruns. On nights when I was unable to sleep I would find myself watching his program, which I felt was funnier than the banal, dated sitcom that preceded it.

In his infomercial he had mostly mediocre mid-to-low level celebrities and quasi-celebrities deliver testimonials about the effectiveness of his program without really giving any details as to how it's done. They just say that their relationships are better, they lost weight, their careers have improved, etc. When the freaky guy speaks for himself, he is rather mum on the particulars of his technique, but pushes his lectures (which have a hefty admission charge, another overlooked detail. I had to investigate to see just how much his tickets were, and was flattened by the price). And not once did he say to work on improving your craft, or be skillful at what you do. He flogs his books and if reading is not your thing, good news: All his books are available on CD! As well, he has other recordings where he sums up motivational and self-improvement books for you written by other New Gurus, so you don't have to be literate to participate in his program, all the while keeping you from buying other people's works.

When I have a chance to talk to followers of the freaky guy, what they say is to me a little disturbing. One such person informed me that the best way to get people to telephone you often is to make sure the first thing you say when answering the phone is that it is so good to hear from the caller, with enthusiasm.

"Even if it is not?" I asked.

They looked at me with bewilderment. "Well … yeah."

"That is just a subtle form of manipulation, don't you think?" I said. "And isn't being manipulative disrespectful, dishonest, and rude to the other person?"

They got uncomfortable and, while they did not acknowledge my point, they did not deny it either.

Another fallacy these New Gurus engage in is the misuse of science for their own gain. They say things like we only use 10% of our brains (not true … that notion is based on a misinterpretation of data that has long since been disproven), or they talk about the importance of playing the role of the alpha wolf (the very notion of the "alpha male wolf" was renounced by the person who coined the term), in an attempt to make their points seem more solid.

They like to quote a legendary football coach, who once said that winning is literally all that matters, as a way of justifying immoral behaviour. That same coach later recanted what he said, saying he was misunderstood; that he meant the struggle and the effort to win is what mattered, and he didn't intend for people to use his words as a license to disregard human decency.

Whenever anyone asks me about what I think of the new generation of motivational speakers, I cite an example from the early 90s and someone (I will refer to said person as "The Hockey Coach") who was such a proud devotee of a New Guru that he appeared in his infomercial. (Before I continue I just want to make one thing clear: I am aware that The Hockey Coach has likely forgotten more about hockey than I will ever know, and I respect that as a former professional player he spent countless hours practicing. I'm not saying I know more than him, or was a better athlete, and I have nothing personal against him; I'm simply creating a composite example of someone who attained a high position not due to their elite skill level, but rather because they knew the right people and were able to sell themselves.)

One of the things I admire about professional sports is that for the most part one can't pretend to be talented or fool people for too long. If you are good at it you will rise. You can't fake scoring a goal, running the fastest, jumping the highest, hitting a home run, throwing a touchdown pass, or delivering a knock-out punch. Sure, you can cheat with illegal substances, tactics, or equipment, but you can't manipulate people into believing you have skills you simply do not have. The stats don't lie. The numbers are there for all to see. Even so, there are exceptions.

In my opinion The Hockey Coach was able to play hundreds of big-league games during his unremarkable career because he was with equally unremarkable teams. After retiring as an active player, he found success as a minor-league coach, winning a championship, and he absolutely deserves credit for that. The next season he was hired to lead a major league team because the owner of said team, a short, stout man who came out of nowhere and curiously made an alleged fortune in a field not renowned for its multi-millionaires, was a devotee of the same guru.

The Hockey Coach was distinguished from his peers because he was relatively young, dynamic, a sharp dresser, and had a mullet (which I'm not criticizing in any way; at the time I had one as well), and although not a top-tier team compared to others in the league at the time, his group was stocked with a smattering of stellar players (although most were no longer in their prime). And once more he merits some credit because he was able to get them into the playoffs, where they over-achieved all the way to the championship finals.

In the semi-finals, The Hockey Coach found himself up against another over-achieving team led by a rather corpulent, veteran major-league bench boss who in seasons past had won the league's coach of the year award. During a heated exchange between benches, the disrespectful younger man ridiculed the other for his excessive girth. The older man took the high road, later saying that being a coach in the big leagues is a fraternity, and The Hockey Coach might himself be on the spot and all alone one day. Then he told him to get a haircut.

The Hockey Coach's opponent in the finals was another former winner of coach of the year with miles more experience, himself a carrier of a few extra pounds, bespectacled with a bad mustache, balding, and as it was later discovered, illiterate, whose team was yet another Cinderella story not expected to get to the finals.

The Hockey Coach's team won game one and led by one goal late in the third period in game two. His opponent called for a stick measure, a common strategy used by coaches in all leagues and at all levels around the world. One of The Hockey Coach's defensemen had an excessive curve on his stick, leading to a two-minute minor penalty. (Most coaches know who has the banned gear and have the presence of mind late in the game to have their offending players switch out when ahead, something The Hockey Coach may have failed to do that time. And they are quite aware of the consequences of not doing so.) On the ensuing power play they were scored on, and again in overtime, costing them game two. They failed to win another in the series and lost the championship.

During the press conference after game two, when asked what he thought of the maneuver, the four flusher did not give any credit to his adversary; he did not say "well, he out-coached me this time, but he won't again!" or something along those lines, which I believe would've been perfectly fine. Instead, he said that he wouldn't want to win that way. Devotees of the New Gurus believe they are the best and brightest guys in the room, and as such they don't take well to setbacks, don't admit to mistakes, belittle the achievements of their rivals, and underestimate said opponents' abilities. Let me get this straight: He would rather win with players using forbidden gear, which sadly is common practice in the league despite being against the rules, but not by employing perfectly legal and accepted tactics used in the past by hall-of-fame coaches.

Eventually the "millionaire" owner of the team went to jail (I believe for fraud) and The Hockey Coach was sacked, not able to duplicate his previous success. He went back to the minors as a coach and broadcaster. After a spell he was able to get hired once again in the majors, this time for a team that was not particularly good; in fact they finished at the bottom of the league the season before and so were able to get a good draft pick the next year, selecting a prospect considered by numerous sportswriters to be the next big thing in hockey.

The Hockey Coach decided not to give his top prospect sufficient ice time, and he and the team floundered. In an interview, The Hockey Coach said that the new player was not ready for the big leagues, not physically mature or strong enough. Soon after, The Hockey Coach found himself on the unemployment line again. And the top prospect? The next coach put him front and centre and playing big minutes. He immediately started scoring and has yet to stop, becoming team captain and winning championships, and possibly, soon after retirement, could find himself in the Hall of Fame.

The New Gurus do not teach people to be good at what they do. They teach them to give the impression they are good at what they do. Their disciples' work is to sell themselves, even after they have the job; to convince others that they do it well, even if they may not. Is that what you want in the professionals you encounter on a daily basis who have the ability to affect your life? Would you accept that from the people teaching your children or the financier who has your retirement fund in their hands? How about the politicians and other elected or appointed public officials who make the decisions and set the policies that impact our daily lives?

They set up meaningless guidelines like "always make eye contact" and convince others of inane "rules" as if those are an excellent way to evaluate a perspective employee, something that especially angers people on the spectrum like myself, who find eye contact difficult and uncomfortable. Believe it or not, it is possible that a person who does not stare at your pupils directly can be a good, competent and capable worker. When I was at the gas station, we were evaluated by surprise mystery customers sent by the huge, faceless oil company. I scored highly on everything but eye contact, and so I didn't achieve a perfect rating. It was so frustrating. People don't understand how difficult it is for me, and those like me-to do that. It makes me even angrier when I think about it now. It's like saying a wheelchair bound employee was not good at his job because he didn't stand at attention when a customer walked into the room.

When you are good at something it is self-evident. That is the best way to sell yourself. Real world results; by working hard, and heeding Steve Martin's advice.

THE GRAND TOUR OF PARK EX

Once upon a mid-April Sunday we didn't get out of bed until around noon. My apartment was dim and had an air of melancholy. When Kay and I stepped out onto my balcony, which overlooked all of TMR, we could see why: It was grey outside. Not cloudy; the sky was not an artful mix of dark and light patches; no swirls of various shades. Just straight flat grey, as though it were covered with battleship paint.

The air was cool and windless. Usually, by that time of year, there were signs of spring's arrival, but the trees and bushes had uncharacteristically not begun to bud; the grass had not a hint of green. It felt like the apocalypse.

We were four weeks into the COVID-19 lockdown, which began the day after my father's funeral. We awoke that morning to find we were now living in a science fiction movie. Watching the alarming news on TV, Kay asked, "What about your job? Do you still have to go back next week?"

As if on cue, my phone rang before I could say I didn't know. It was my boss, telling me that the bookstore was closing down for the foreseeable future and that I was going to be laid off.

I was surviving on U.I. and we were splitting our time between my place and Kay's. Sleeping in and teaming up to cook elaborate meals became our thing, as well as long afternoon walks, and evenings watching movies and bingeing TV shows. I introduced her to the various *Star Trek* series, which she took to, and she insisted I watch *The Crown* and to tell the truth, I ended up loving it.

"What do you want to do today, sweetie?" she asked.

"Let's take a walk."

"Where?"

"Have you ever been around Park Ex? I mean *really* seen the place?"

Kay had lived in Montreal since her student days, mostly downtown or in Mile End, and although she had been to Park Ex, it was to her mostly unfamiliar territory.

"No."

"Then please allow me the honour of taking you on The Grand Tour of Park Ex."

After our late breakfast, we left on foot and headed east towards the neighbouring Park Extension district. We took the pedestrian bridge over the railroad tracks and zig-zagged our way through the treed and mostly empty streets of TMR, a municipality whose roadways radiate out like a spider's web from the town center, a one-time country club.

It didn't take us long to get to one of the gates on the tree- and bush-lined Selwood Road that opens onto Park Ex. We took the one at Jarry, which gave us easy access to the places I lived, growing up. We crossed L'Acadie Boulevard and headed towards Wiseman Avenue and Jarry where the Station 5 taxi stand is located.

At that intersection, there is now an Indian restaurant that was, when I was young, a pizzeria called The Corner Restaurant that doubled as a cabbie hangout. It was the spot where all the Greek drivers for Champlain Taxi had their little clique as they sat around, drank coffee, smoked cigarettes, and talked while waiting for fares. That was where I went to visit with my dad after the divorce. Standing at that spot awakened countless memories.

* * *

The first to come to mind was when I went to see Dad who, with a smile on his face, told me that my grandfather had died. I'm sure he wasn't happy about it, but there was no real tragedy; his father was in his nineties after all, and died peacefully in his sleep. In fact he told me that when his mother awoke in the middle of the night and found her husband of over seventy years dead, she simply rolled over and went back to sleep. She got up at her usual time the next day and called the authorities. When I asked Dad when he died, he said a few days ago.

"Why didn't you call me right away?"

"Ahh!" Dad said, waving his hand.

A similar scenario was repeated when my grandmother died.

The oddest incident happed when I went to see Dad and he had a beat-up old manila envelope that contained an equally beat-up old book. His younger brother Gus had sent it to him to give to me. I was unsure why, since I've not once met Uncle Gus or so much as spoken to or corresponded with him. Dad explained that Gus was deep into astrology and numerology, and I was the only close relative he had with the same zodiac sign, so he felt we had some sort of metaphysical connection or something.

The book was titled *Self Mastery and Fate with the Cycles of Life* by H. Spencer Lewis. A sticker on the inside cover indicated that it was originally purchased at the Aquarian Book Centre (my uncle and I are, coincidentally enough, both Aquarians), 26 Van Der Merwe Street in a neighbourhood called Hillbrow, in Johannesburg, South Africa.

Gus had left Greece as a young man to seek his fortune, first going to Brazil with another brother and one of his cousins. When that didn't work out he settled alone in South Africa, where he became a successful electrical contractor and a high-roller (my father told me his brother was such a gambler that he would call casinos and they would send a helicopter for him when he was ready to game). The only one of my father's siblings to neither marry nor have children.

There is an old family story told to me by one of my relatives about the time Gus and his cousin visited a high-class casino. Upon arrival Gus gave said cousin half his cash with the strict instructions that, no matter what, he was not to give him that portion of the money. Not an hour later Gus had an unbreakable grip on his cousin's lapels, violently shaking him and screaming: "Give me my money! Forget what I said! Give it to me! Goddammit, give it to me!"

My uncle ultimately returned to Greece an old man, single, childless and penniless. He died not long after I received the book. Although I am not unappreciative of his gift, I have yet to read it; I mean, look at the luck it brought him.

It was at Station 5 that Dad and I had a defining talk. He was angry at me because of my refusal to attend one of my cousins' wedding. I was unsure why he cared so much, because it was a cousin on my mother's side, and this was more than a decade after my parents' divorce. Dad did not buy my excuse.

"You are such an enigma," he said, in Greek. "What the hell is wrong with you? Want to know why half of your relatives don't like you? Why half of everyone doesn't like you? This is why!"

"No," I said, "that's not it."

"What is it, then?"

"Well, let me ask you: All the people you know, relatives or not, who like me. What kind of people are they?"

"They are intelligent, kind, pleasant people with a sense of humour."

"And the people who don't?"

"Angry, humourless, bitter, mean, usually not particularly bright ..."

"So why is it my fault? Why am *I* the problem?"

"Ahh," he said, with a quick wave of his hand. He didn't come up with an answer.

My father spent most of his time at Station 5. So much so that when I was Best Man at The Weasel's wedding, his bride's older brother Vladimir, who had not met my father before, told me that when he would get off the 80 bus at Jarry and walk home to the family residence on Stuart, he would pass the taxi stand and usually see my Dad there. I told him to tell that to Dad. When he heard that, Dad said: "Yes! That *eez* true!" and laughed gregariously, as only he could.

Once I went to see Dad on a sunny summer day. He was third in a line of taxis that wasn't moving. It looked like a slow afternoon. We sat and talked and smoked cigarettes, when I noticed a plastic bag lying on his back seat that he must have overlooked. I brought it to his attention. He grabbed the bag, which was from a pharmacy. It contained three syringes labelled "methadone" and a black, egg-shaped cellular flip-phone. (This was long before they had become ubiquitous.)

"Ahh," Dad said, "it *eez* from that *kolopetho* (bum-child). He *eez* a *djunkee*."

Just at that moment, the cell phone rang. I answered it. On the other end was someone who sounded young with a Park Ex Greek accent. I explained that the person he was trying to call had left his phone and "medicine" in a taxi and he should contact said friend on his landline and tell him to call his cell if he wants his shit back.

Not two minutes later the phone's owner called. My father took the call and spoke to him in Greek, telling him to come to the stand to collect his bag. He refused. My father then said he did not want to lose his place in line and would bring it to him for $5.

I went with him to return the bag. The Junkie lived between D'Anvers and Jarry on the bottom floor of a triplex, I'd assume with one or both of his parents. He came onto his balcony, wearing only jogging pants and flip-flops. He had a muscular upper torso, but by the way his leggings were hanging he looked like he should sue his lower limbs for lack of support. My father stopped his car and waved for him to come to us, but The Junkie became belligerent, a behaviour that did not surprise me.

"Fuck you, old man!" he said to my dad. "Come here for your fuckin' money!"

I undid my seat belt and was about to get out but Dad waved me off. He got out and exchanged the bag for the cash. When they stood next to each other I saw that The Junkie was an inch or two shorter than Dad, himself no champ in the height department.

As Dad turned to leave, The Junkie said, "Next time I call for a cab I'll tell them not to send you!"

Dad just waved him off and walked away.

As we drove back to the taxi stand I thought about how much crap Dad had to put up with on a daily basis to make a living.

"What an asshole," I said.

"Ahh, forget *heem*. He *eez djust* an *axristos djunkie*."

We went back to the stand and continued our conversation. He had a large, heavy flashlight hanging from a screw he had driven into his dashboard. I picked it up and turned it on. It didn't light up.

"Hey, your flashlight doesn't work."

"Can you *stheel* use *eet* to smash someone's head *een*?" Dad said.

"I guess."

"Then *eet stheel werkin*!"

I didn't ask Dad if that incident was what finally convinced him to retire or if he simply felt like it was time, but a few months later when I visited him at Station 5 he announced his retirement. He was seventy, soon to be seventy-one, and told me he had found a buyer for his car and taxi permit. At first, I wondered if he was ill because in the past he told me that he would resist retiring, instead opting to simply slow down, like his father, who worked the family farm until the day he died. Dad looked significantly thinner, and, when I asked, he assured me his health was good and that he was on a new diet to lose weight.

"I am in *thee* good shape," he said. "*Thee* doctor told me to stop *thee shoogarz* and *thee cheegarette*. I can stop eating anything but I *weel* not give up *thee bif*. I love *thee bif*! I will do what he say. I don't care *eef* I die tomorrow, I *djust* don't want to be *seek*."

Dad did get sick and the last years of his life were spent battling a long list of ailments, including Parkinson's disease and dementia. Visiting him at his home during that time was difficult. The robust and sociable man I knew growing up was slipping away, and conversations with him, once vibrant and interesting, were now a challenge.

Late in his illness, I went to see him to talk about how much it bothered me that he would let his friend Argethis, whom I called *Archidias* (Greek for testicles), walk all over me with impunity when I was younger. When I mentioned him, Dad, eyes glassy with an indifferent look on his face, simply said in Greek: "He was not a good friend. He died eight years ago. Last few years he only called when he wanted money or something ..." without really addressing my question. I don't know if he didn't understand me because I asked in English, or if he just didn't get what I wanted to know. I felt it fitting that *Archidias* died friendless, drunk, and broke. Still, I wish I could have told him off myself.

* * *

Kay and I continued down to Wiseman where I showed her my old school, Barclay Elementary. They had recently built an extension at the rear of the mammoth building.

"When I was a student here," I told Kay, "there was a wood and aluminum structure at the back called 'The Annex.' It was where the Grade 6 kids were. They built it as a temporary measure because the school was overcrowded. When I started school I couldn't wait to have classes there. It meant you were one of the seniors. But I didn't get my chance."

"What happened?"

"Well, enrollment in English schools had been steadily declining since the language laws were enacted in the mid-70s. I myself went to a French-language pre-kindergarten until the law was amended to allow students to go to English schools if they had an older sibling who was being educated in English. The year I was to start Grade 6 they tore it down. My brother told me I was lucky; he had Grade 6 in The Annex and said it was small, overcrowded, too hot or too cold, and the air was perpetually stale. There was a rumour that it was full of asbestos. But that was just a rumour."

When we got to Ball and Wiseman, I gave Kay a quick history of the now-iconic Marven's Restaurant and how it had such a decidedly non-Greek moniker: It was originally a corner store owned by a man named "Marven." When I was just a kid my mom would sometimes send my brother and me there, to buy milk or butter. Marven sold it to a Hellenic family that slowly converted it into a souvlaki place. At first, it was half store, half restaurant, and within two years the store part was completely gone. The family liked to hunt big game animals and the décor inside was full of stuffed deer, moose, coyotes, and other hairy mammals in a macabre zoo that would make Norman Bates jealous. Eventually most of the taxidermy was removed.

Pre-COVID there were lineups to get in during the summer with people coming from all over to eat there. When I lived on the corner of Stuart and Ball or Wiseman and St. Roch, it was not uncommon for me to be stopped on the street and asked for directions to the renowned Park Ex eatery.

As the tour continued we caught sight of a young man in his 20s riding a unicycle. It was indicative of how the neighbourhood was changing, and younger, artier types and college students were slowly moving to Park Ex with the new campus of the Université de Montréal, just over the railroad tracks. When I was a kid, if an unfortunate soul were to try to express any form of individuality by riding around on a unicycle, the local toughs, who would have none of that, would chase them down, beat them up, and break the unicycle to pieces before their eyes. Today, a person could ride around the streets with impunity. (I am of course neither endorsing violent behaviour nor implying that they *should* have been beaten up … just that they *would* have been.)

I pointed in the direction of Birnam Street where my family lived for two years when I was a child. I recounted the time a guy my mother knew from the old country, a cousin of her brother-in-law, had come to Canada as an immigrant and worked at my uncle's restaurant. He ran into some immigration trouble, and a quick marriage was arranged with a Greek-born woman who had her citizenship. My father drove him to the church on Sherbrooke and St. Laurent (the same church where I was baptized, which, like all Greek houses of worship, suffered the shared fate of burning to the ground), for his wedding, with my mom, brother and myself in the back seat. The guy was getting cold feet, and babbling about how he was riddled with doubts about the whole deal. Exasperated, my father put a quick end to it all when he said (in Greek), "What, *rhé*!?! She's a woman! Just take her!" Their marriage outlasted my parents' union by decades.

We strolled along Ball Avenue, headed east, when we came across Bloomfield and Ball, and that evoked another memory: When I was in my late teens I went to my father's apartment, which was all the way at the other end of Park Ex, to pick up my tuition fee for Dawson College. We talked for a bit and he offered to drive me home. I didn't mind walking but he said he was going back to work anyway, so I figured "why not?"

At the aforementioned intersection, my father slammed on the brakes when he saw this old man with a cane gradually inching his way down the street, and yelled, "Hey, Tommy! It's me! George! Need a ride?" Then Dad quickly turned to me and said, "Get out! Get out now!" which I did, quite confused. Tommy got into the back of Dad's cab and they drove off.

Later that night my Dad called to apologize. "Andreas," he said, "sorry but he *geeves* you $20 *djust* to take *heem* to *thee leeker* commission on *Djean-Dalon* and back."

"That's okay. Twenty bucks is twenty bucks," I said, admittedly a little miffed that Dad would boot me out of his car for an old drunk.

We continued to St. Roch and what I call "The Big Blue Church," where weeks earlier we'd had my father's service.

* * *

The years had caught up with Dad in his eighties, and no diet or medicine was going to help him anymore. One night when I was at work my brother called and said Dad had fallen. They were now at the emergency department at the Jewish General Hospital. Luckily enough for me, I took the 165 bus to go home and it went right past there. I went after work to find Peter and my father's current wife by his bedside. Dad did not seem hurt but was disoriented. They had been there for hours. I told them I would take the night shift.

Dad was in and out of comprehension. He spoke Greek, then classical Greek, then a little English. The hospital did not give him anything to eat so I went and bought him a muffin and watched him slowly ingest it. Then he told me a meandering tale of how he first came to Canada: Greece was in a crippling recession. As Dad described it, "I *deed* not have enough *mah-knees* for *thee cheegarette*!"

Out of the navy after a four-year stint and broke, he went to Hamburg, Germany to look for work on merchant ships. There were a number of Greeks already there, looking for work; people the Germans callously dismissed as "wogs." Dad joked that he walked around looking up at the much taller Germans, fearful that they would step on him.

He signed onto a merchant freighter and for years he got to see the world. A fateful voyage to Madagascar to get raw sugar changed his life. His ship then went to the Port of Montreal to unload and reload, this time with wheat. It was then that my father and a friend of his jumped ship and began their Canadian lives. Dad lived here without legal status for years until he was blackmailed into his first disastrous marriage to avoid deportation, and in time attained full citizenship.

* * *

A social worker determined that my father's wife could not properly take care of him anymore and they sought to place him in a chronic care facility for the aged.

Fortunately, they found one close to where they lived and my father's wife visited him all day, every day, keeping him company, feeding him his meals, doing his laundry, and continuing to take care of him. We should all be so blessed as to have someone in our lives as devoted to us as she was to him, especially since I feel that had the tables been turned he would not have returned the favour.

My father's attitude towards *thee woo-manz* was, to say the least, a little old-fashioned. I could imagine his wife getting sick and he would dump her on her daughter's doorstep, ring the doorbell, and then high-tail it out of there. By the time her daughter opened the front door, Dad would be peeling away in his car yelling to her: "*Djust* call me for *thee foon-eral* … *weetch* I am *NOT* paying for!"

At the funeral, he would arrive for the service late, leave early, and bring a date.

There is precedent for that in his family. One of my father's relatives, who resided in Greece, once met a Scandinavian tourist, had a whirlwind romance with her, and got married within a few months. Then she brought him to her home country to meet the kin. Big mistake. He immediately fell in love with his new wife's sister, who was already married and had a small child. Guess what? The sister fell for his charms as well and they ran off together. It is said that when he brought her to his hometown and she met my grandparents, they were shocked because she wore pants (my grandmother had worn nothing but dresses her entire life), and she knew how to drive a car.

In the early 90s, I met them in Greece and stayed at their house. I saw nothing but a loving couple in a three-decade plus happy marriage. A few years later she fell ill and died. My father felt that news was so unimportant that he didn't tell me until way after the fact. What did my father's relative do? According to my father, he refused to pay for her burial, going to her family and demanding that *they* pay for it. Unsurprisingly, they refused. I was told he had the nerve to try (unsuccessfully) to get his first wife to come back to him. (I have to be fair to him: This information was third-hand, so I can't attest to its accuracy. On top of that one must consider he was by no means a wealthy man and perhaps wanted to give her a more elaborate funeral than he could afford on his own; and how afraid, desperate, and insecure would any of us be if we lost our partner of over thirty years? What acts would any of us be capable of?)

Old-fashioned Greek guys probably believe there should be a drop-off place where one could dump their expired *woo-manz*, after sewing their bodies into a burlap sack, for a free burial in a mass grave. I can imagine a place à la *Soylent Green* that had a drive-thru with a large conveyor belt where they would drop off the deceased and speed away quickly to a nudie bar with a name like "Big Bill's Booby Hatch."

* * *

We continued on to Ogilvy Avenue where CFCF TV was once located, on a site at the edge of Park Ex. When I was young there used to be a small theatre (the Empire Cinema) on the corner of Ogilvy and Durocher that played Greek movies and later housed the Hellenic Federation of Montreal. We would go there for matinees some Saturdays and Sundays. Once during Easter when I was about five or six they were showing a movie about the crucifixion. My mother brought me and my brother to see it along with one of her sisters and some of her brood. As we walked home at night Mom asked me if I believed in Jesus. I knew she would be pleased if I said yes, so I did, not knowing or understanding what I was agreeing to. Mom has since taken it as a lifelong commitment on my part; to this day she continues to refer to that night, as I point out that my answer was made under duress and didn't constitute a legally binding contract.

* * *

Then we crossed back towards TMR and passed the mortuary where we had Dad's viewing.

* * *

I saw my father at the seniors' residence Saturdays in the late afternoon, often giving his wife a ride back to her condo after visiting hours were over. Then one Saturday I came and found Dad unresponsive and breathing with the aid of a respirator. My cousin Johnny B. was there with his girlfriend and mother. When they left my aunt took my father's wife outside with her to give us a moment alone, and I said my goodbyes. I put my hand on his head and told him I loved him. Then I left.

I stayed over at Kay's that night. The next day I went to work. At 12:30 pm, I had my lunch and checked the messages on my phone. My brother had left an urgent voicemail telling me he was at the residence and I should come to see Dad, saying he did not have much time left. I immediately called and he told me Dad had died peacefully with his wife, brother, sister, nephew, stepchildren, and step-grandchildren all there with him.

When I spoke to Peter they were waiting for the mortuary to take him away, which took a while because COVID was gaining traction and there were a lot of deceased people at chronic care facilities to pick up. In fact, I was told that when they arrived the van was almost at capacity and Dad was not their exclusive pickup. I asked if I should go there and he told me not to bother.

I called my boss and he gave me the week off to take care of things. I called Kay and told her the news. I asked her if I could come over. She said yes.

Monday morning I went shopping for a white shirt and black tie.

Tuesday we had an all-day viewing. Because our relationship at that point was fairly new I told Kay she could skip it but I wanted and needed her to be there with me the next day for the funeral.

The viewing was a long but satisfying day; quite a few people came to pay tribute to Dad. The sad thing was that he was eighty-eight years old, and most of his best friends, the ones who would have paid the best tributes and knew who he truly was, were already gone. My aunt brought a pen and a book of Greek crossword puzzles to put in the casket. Dad loved doing crosswords.

The funeral was held at the Big Blue Church where Dad's wife had a religious ceremony despite the fact that he was a lifelong atheist, but I did not object. Dad had told me before he died that it was all right for her to do what she wanted.

In her life, Kay had not been to a Greek Orthodox service and was unprepared for what was about to unfold. We entered the church and they set up Dad's open casket at the front.

While I regularly say that the Greek Orthodox Church has all the disadvantages of Catholicism with none of the advantages of Protestantism, I do tell people they have to attend at least one Greek Orthodox *Panikhida* (memorial service). Despite abhorring the fact that they do not allow for eulogies or anything personal or particular to the deceased, it is still a spectacle worthy of a Broadway production.

All was quiet. We lit our candles, and the show began.

A curtain at the back of the altar opened and two priests and a *psalti* (cantor) came out. They began the elaborate ceremony of chants, incense and prayers that lasted continuously for about twenty minutes. There were no flubs, pauses or errors. When it was over, all three men went back through the stage door and closed the curtains.

"Wow," Peter said, surprised that portions of the ceremony were in English, observing how they didn't do that when we were kids. "That was cool!"

We concurred.

My father, if he were there, would have had a good laugh at the whole thing, believing religion to be the biggest joke of all. I'm surprised he didn't rise up to curse out the priests in front of the entire congregation. Even more surprising was that, when they draped his body with the flag of the Orthodox Church before closing the casket for the last time, it did not burst into flames on contact with his skin.

The procession went to Mount Royal Cemetery for interment, where my uncle, now the last of the Kessaris brothers of Meligalas, had some beautiful final words for his older sibling, ending with "…they say we all go through the same doors. If that's true we see you again, my brother."

We then returned to the Big Blue Church's basement for coffee.

My friend Les was there to pay her respects, as were a handful of relatives from my mother's side of the family. At one point an old man walked up to me to express his sympathies.

"Do you remember me?" he asked.

"Sorry, I don't."

Then he reminded me:

In the mid-90s my father and the woman that would be his final in a series of wives moved into a condo just off L'Acadie, north of Sauvé. They had all new appliances, including a huge refrigerator, the kind with a long freezer on the left side.

They often spent their summers in Greece, and Dad would give me the keys to his pad to water the plants on their balcony, telling me to make sure that I didn't over-water them because his neighbour downstairs would complain like a whiny bitch if so much as a drop fell on his balcony. I went there weekly to water the plants and one time when I wasn't paying close attention I accidentally did exactly what I was told not to do. The next week there was an angry note on the door of my father's apartment, the condescending wording of which made me want to go downstairs and staple the note to the guy's forehead. *How dare he talk to my dad like that?* But instead, I had an idea. I left the note on the door, and this time purposely overwatered. I continued to do the same each time and the note remained there. If the guy went up to complain he would realize they were away and perhaps think it was someone else's fault. A few weeks later the note was gone. The downstairs jerk probably heard that they were away and took his poisoned letter back, wondering who was really responsible for that unforgivable offense.

Moreover, Dad had told me that a friend of his would be contacting me to collect something from their place and I should let him in.

He called a few weeks later and I met him at the condo. My dad did not tell me what he was going to retrieve, and I was dying to know. When we entered the unit he went straight for their freezer. He opened it up and took out two long, thick slabs of meat, frozen solid as granite.

"What's that?" I asked.

"*Eet eez thee* prime *reeb*," he said.

"What are you going to do with that?"

"I am going right now to *thee* airport. I am taking *eet* with me to Greece."

"What's it doing here?"

"Your father is *thee* only *pear-son* I know who have *thee beeg* freezer."

"Won't it thaw by the time it gets there?"

"No," he said, "*eet eez* totally frozen. *Eet* not melt for days."

"That seems like a lot of trouble to go through. I've been to Greece. They have meat there, eh."

He sighed and looked directly at me, waving his hand for emphasis and saying: "Yes. I know. But they do not have *thee* prime *reeb*! I am going to cook *theess* for a wedding."

Fair enough. Greeks smuggled things in and out of Greece. My father came home from such trips with a suitcase full of carefully hidden bottles of Metaxa and cartons of Karelia cigarettes. When he could he would smuggle the cactus pears he loved that grow wild all over Greece, bars of *pasteli* (a chewy, sesame seed and honey snack food) and cans of thick, dark unpasteurized honey. Dad swore by the honey from his hometown, saying that it was a kind of superfood. He would claim that it built strong muscles and had healing properties because the bees use it as food and medicine. (For Mom, extra virgin olive oil from Greece and aspirin were her cure-alls, as well as a natural tea made from wildflowers.)

* * *

Kay and I crossed L'Acadie at Ogilvy and re-entered TMR. By now the light had gone and we went home for supper. The Grand Tour was over.

* * *

A year later Kay and I found ourselves at my place again, waking up late and discussing what we should do on that sunny and cold afternoon.

"Have they put your father's stone up yet? Have you visited his grave since the burial?" she asked.

I texted Peter and sure enough, he said the stone was up. So we decided to visit Mount Royal Cemetery.

"Do you want to bring something? Some flowers maybe?" she said.

I thought about it ... *what would Dad say about that?*

An aggressive image popped into my head of Dad yelling at me, "*Ti kanis, esei*!?! (What are you doing?) *Thee mens* don't buy flowers for *thee* other *mens*! *Ti esai esei, san tôh* Jody *apo tôh Soap*?!?(What are you, like Jody from *Soap*?) Why you waste *thee mah-nees* on *thee* flowers!?!"

"Ah, no. Not flowers. We'll see," I said.

We drove up and with the help of an app, we found Dad's final resting place. The stone was a cross with my father's picture embedded in it, along with an image of the Virgin Mary. All his wife's doing. Fair enough. And again, Dad said she could do what she wanted, but those were all things my father would not have accepted. Add to that his last name was misspelled in Greek.

People had visited the site recently and tied flowers and candles to the modest monument.

Kay and I stood there. Then I had an idea. In my trunk I had a few copies of *The Butcher of Park Ex*. My aunt told me that Dad had lamented before he died that his one great regret in life was that he would not live long enough to hold a copy of my book, being published the following October, in his hands before dying. And it bothered me that he didn't get to see it with his own eyes. So I retrieved a copy, and placed it on the stone, secured by a binding that held some flowers. Then I took a photo of it and posted the shot on my social media.

Now I'm not a believer in the afterlife; I know Dad is not floating around like Casper the Ghost watching what we do. People instantly started messaging me or commenting on the post saying that Dad is probably reading the book in heaven. Don't get me wrong. I greatly appreciate the sentiment, but knowing and understanding my father as I did, and seeing as how his favourite movie was *Porky's*, if there is life after death then he is out there somewhere visiting women's locker rooms.

That being said, placing my book there did surprisingly give me a feeling of peace. And a sense of closure.

SEND IN THE FUCKING CLOWNS

I was thirty-eight when the realization hit me that I'd spent my life living with older relatives, and hadn't had my name on a lease one single time, or on a mortgage or deed. Now I was completely free of debt. I was finally on my way and, after fourteen years, ready to get my life going. At last I was working a job in a field where I belonged; I had employment that I was not constantly on the edge of quitting. No more false starts. No more deferrals. No more excuses. It was time.

The first time I moved out was when I was twenty. My mother was going to remarry and wanted me out of the house. I was about to go to university and by chance Peter had a place near campus and his roommate was moving out to join the army. He was apprehensive of finding someone that he did not know well, and I could not afford a place on my own. By the time I graduated Peter wanted to move in with his girlfriend, and I moved back in with Mom.

I sometimes looked for work outside of Montreal, so I figured why bother getting a place that would tie me down and keep me from just getting up and going, should the opportunity strike, but said opportunities didn't materialize.

Over the years I flirted with the idea of buying a condo, or spoke about cohabitating with a girlfriend or potential roommate, but that seldom went past the theoretical stage. Now I was ready and I knew what I wanted. Starting a family was probably not in the cards for me, so I was not going to buy any property. My reasoning at the time was, why bother if I have no one to leave it to when I was old or gone? Upkeep and repairs were on another person's nickel. Renting was the option for me.

I had no idea how to seriously do that, and the most recent vicarious experience I had had at the time was my brother's search for an apartment after he broke up with his girlfriend. Peter had bought a house in rural La Plaine, way out of Montreal, to start a family. When the relationship failed, he sold the small cottage and wanted to move back to the island. He first found a dingy ground-floor apartment on Birnam just north of Liège that I called "the cave," a depressing hole that had no balcony, and the gloomy shadow cast by the surrounding row houses kept the sun from finding any of his windows all year round. He began looking for a better place in the neighbourhood but ran into landlords who preferred renting to families. Mom found him a place on L'Acadie between Ball and Jarry, but the sanctimonious Greek asshole who owned the building balked when he found out that my brother was a single parent, which to the landlord was morally objectionable. Even worse, the child they had was out of wedlock, and to top it all off, the child's mother was not Greek.

To me the landlord/tenant relationship is rather nonsensical: It is one of the few financial transactions where the customer is perpetually in the wrong; the only one where you give the bulk of your earnings to someone and they treat you like shit; as though having to fulfill their contractual and legal obligations was a painful burden. When I was young all the renters in Park Ex referred to their landlords as their "Boss." It harkened back to the old country where tenant farmers worked for the owner of the land in exchange for harsh rent and a share of the crops grown. I heard tales of how there were few legal recourses for the cottiers, who were constantly under the threat of eviction and subjected to constant harassment and outlandish rate increases. That couldn't possibly happen here in this day and age, could it? (That's why I feel tenants should be protected not by provincial rental boards, but by a federal law similar to a consumer protection act.)

Peter finally found a great second-floor place on Stuart, not far from where we grew up, that he loved, was affordable, and had a balcony, and the icing on the cake was it had good solar orientation. He lived there for years, only to be reno-victed after a new campus of the Université de Montréal was erected just over the railroad tracks from Park Ex, and his greedy landlords sensed that they could get a tad more money monthly by leasing the property to students from out of town on a more short-term basis, or as an Air B&B. In the end the joke was on them because the year the new campus was supposed to open COVID hit and classes went virtual, with most university students opting to stay home and few people travelling.

Despite knowing all of that I was still unprepared for the task that lay ahead of me.

I began easily enough by taking long walks around Park Ex and jotting down numbers from the "á *louer*" signs that I came across. I didn't make enough for a large place and I didn't want to buy a fridge, stove, or other pricey appliances and get myself back in debt; semi-furnished with a laundry room in the building was the way to go, hopefully with a garage or parking space for my motorized vehicle.

I found what looked like a reasonable place on D'Anvers Avenue in Park Ex. When I called the number on the sign I was told they did not have anything available for another nine months, and even then it was only one place.

"Well, so why do you have the 'for rent' sign up, then, if you are not renting right now?" I asked.

They hung up on me.

All my life I have resided between Decarie Boulevard and The Main, the mountain and the Metropolitan. That small, centralized, densely populated area, with access to all one would need and not far from downtown, is the greatest piece of real estate on Earth if you ask me. But desperation was setting in, so I began to look at other neighbourhoods.

I took my car around the Villeray-St. Michel area looking for a residence that could work for me. I noticed that some buildings on Christophe-Colomb and Jarry were being renovated. Their huge billboards advertised that they were looking for tenants, so I took down the number and called a few times, but I was unable to get anyone, just voice mail. I left a message saying I was interested in renting one of their units. I didn't get a callback. A few days later I called again. And again. They didn't reply. Not one time.

So I started to look at the Town of Mount Royal, the suburb right next to Park Ex. It is a fancy, upper-middle-class-to-wealthy neighbourhood, but I decided to give it a go anyway. The center of town is a circle with a number of lovely, charming buildings. All had signs outside advertising apartments. I took down numbers and called. When I left messages they did not call back. When I got a live person on the phone they either had no vacancies (again my curiosity compelled me to ask why they had signs up if they had no available units…and again they would hang up on me), or the places were way out of my price range.

I tried looking downtown. More expensive, but I could walk to work, thus saving me the cost of a monthly transit pass. The only place that had parking was the massive and declining La Cité complex, but none of their rental units interested me.

I later went to the more prestigious Rockhill apartments in Côte-des-Neiges. I was in the office of the building manager, a small, friendly, white-haired, grandmotherly woman, who told me they had a studio opening up soon. She quoted me a price I felt was a little too steep. July 1st is the traditional moving day in Montreal, and it was opening up off-season. Thinking I could negotiate a better price because they could have difficulty renting the place, and because at the time there was a tenant-friendly vacancy rate on the Island of Montreal, I decided to try some wheeling-dealing.

"Well," I said, "I found a similar apartment for less at La Cité …"

"Don't compare me to *La Cité*!" she said. "Don't you dare compare me to *La Cité*!"

She stood up and asked me to leave.

"Humph," she said as I exited. "*La Cité. Really*!?!"

I started patrolling the Borough of Ville St. Laurent. It is north of the Met but with good access to public transit. On my first day looking I came across a six-floor apartment building just off of Côte-Vertu and within walking distance of the Deux-Montagnes commuter train that went directly downtown. I took out my phone and called the number on the sign outside. To my shock not only did a living, breathing person answer, but he was friendly and ready to show me an available apartment that second.

I met The Super at the door. He appeared glad to see me, greeting my arrival with a warm smile. He was a thin English-speaking man in late middle age with blue eyes and grey hair. He was eager to show me a 3½ that he was fixing up that would be ready in just a few weeks. When we went to the elevator, a young South Asian family exited. He bid them a jovial, pleasant good day and they smiled at him. I took that as a good sign; he was not racist and not only allowed ethnics into the building but liked their presence.

"Where do you live now?" he said.

"Park Ex."

"I managed a building there a few years back," he said. "It was on Bloomfield and St. Roch. It was filled with troublemakers. In fact, you know that bar on St. Roch around the corner from there? When it closed at 3 am they used to continue the party in one of the apartments. I kept calling the police on them until they moved out. Cleaned the place up, and now there are good, hard-working immigrant families there. We had a similar problem at this place. The bad eggs here, they gathered in the parking garage to do drugs, but I kept calling the cops and now they are all gone. Just good families. Clean living, decent people."

The Super showed me the apartment; I liked it and it was affordable. Freshly painted. Appliances. Balcony. It was ideal for me. I asked if I could see the parking garage.

"Well, you will have to park on the street until a space opens up," he said, "but wait, maybe there is something I can do."

I could tell he really wanted me in the building. It felt good to be a desirable tenant, especially after all the hang-ups and unreturned calls.

He brought me to the garage and showed me a small space.

"Your car fit there?" he asked.

"I'm afraid not," I said.

"How about this? I take out some of this clutter here on one side, and ask this guy to move his car over a foot or two. Would that work?"

"Sure," I said, ready to fill out my credit form and sign the lease.

"Great."

We went to his office and he gave me the forms. Then he pulled a pamphlet out of his jacket pocket.

"Here, have this," he said, handing it to me.

I looked at the cover. It was a pamphlet for Christianity. Instantly, images of that fanatic poking his nose in my business, his eyes judging me if I had a woman over, or perhaps going through my apartment when I'm not there to make sure I don't have any contraband in my place ran through my head.

"I'll … I'll fill out the forms and bring them back to you tomorrow," I said, and beat a hasty retreat, speeding away in my car as quickly as I could.

The following Monday I was taking the 80 bus to work and ran into Marty, an old buddy of mine from my banking days. I told him what had transpired, and he had the best line about situations like that: "Nothing good ever happens after someone hands you one of those fucking things."

I decided to try TMR again, this time one of the buildings that line the Met between Rockland Road and Decarie on Côte-de-Liesse, across from the old National Film Board of Canada complex. On Glengarry Street, I discovered a pleasant brown brick apartment block that it turned out was owned by one of my former clients from my days at branch. He set me up with a roomy 3½ on the top floor that faced away from the highway, had a large, private, covered balcony, a fridge & stove, heating, A/C, and an indoor parking space. He was so hot to have me there he cut me a deal on the rent. I loved the place the first moment I saw it. The panoramic view encompassed the entire north face of the mountain and included the Université de Montréal engineering tower, St. Joseph's Oratory, and if you looked far enough east, the top of the Olympic Stadium tower. During the summer the fireworks shows from the Old Port were visible. I had to wait four months before I could move in, but I wanted the apartment, signing the lease as soon as I passed the credit check.

From my balcony I overlooked picturesque TMR with its green canopy. During the summer, the moon rose over the mountain so large I could see, with the naked eye, the great glowing orb's craters. When there was a thunderstorm the spectacle was amazing, and I had an ideal perch to see immense, colourful rainbows when the tempest was over.

For over a decade that apartment was my bachelor pad. I liked it so much that on multiple occasions I'd find myself giggling with giddy delight and saying aloud, "I have such a cool apartment!" as I jumped for joy and danced a jig like a ninny.

Then things started to go bad. It began when some of the neighbours I had had for years moved away or died and were occasionally being replaced by more transient people. It was as though the faces were constantly changing, to the point where I think the owner of the building had started leasing units with Airbnb, or another similar company. Then they rented to a drug dealer, and almost overnight a crime wave hit our residence. Where once it was quiet, now junkies were roaming the halls, knocking on doors looking for the right apartment. Cars were being broken into. There was vandalism. Things like that just didn't happen in our building, mostly occupied by families and retirees. Eventually, after six months of turmoil, the cops raided the guy and instantly it was over. But the damage was done and a number of people had left. Then the long-time building manager, someone you could talk to and who was helpful and friendly, retired and was replaced by someone who was difficult and decidedly unfriendly, adversarial, and confrontational.

Time went on and I began a relationship that changed my life. Kay and I decided to live together and we began searching for a place just right for us. My bachelor days behind me, I was ready to move to another place, though based on the way things were going, I probably would have done that in time, even if I had not begun seeing her.

Kay and I sat down and went over the ground rules: what we wanted, what we needed, what we didn't want, and where we wanted to live. We agreed to a VETO clause, i.e. at any time one of us could refuse a place for any reason with no questions asked, and the matter had to be dropped right then and there: No "I told you so's" or other hard feelings.

Kay, who had way more experience than I when it came to apartment hunting, usually found the places online and we went looking on weekends and evenings. She wanted to stay in the Mile End neighbourhood where she had lived for over ten years. I was flexible but needed an area with decent street parking if the apartment didn't come with a space.

Growing up in the 70s, the Mile End/Plateau district had a reputation of being a bit of a seedy area. The immigrant families who made up the populace had moved on to suburbs, leaving behind mostly the dregs. In the late 80s students and artists were attracted to the area by its low rents and prime location and it was reborn as a trendy, overrated district with overpriced specialty shops and of course, a Lululemon. (However a few places, like Serrano's Chicken, remain authentic.) It became an area of life coaches, reiki practitioners, maternity doulas, and influencers. Say what one will about drug dealing and bank robbing, at least those are *real* jobs.

The Mile End/Plateau area after gentrification is, to me at least, best summed up by a diner on one if its large streets that was completely renovated a few years ago. A number of people recommended it as a great place for breakfast. So I went there. The food was cold, the portions were small, the service was lousy, and the cost was high. My preferred diner is a more authentic place in Montreal's North End called Paulo & Suzanne. Harder to get to, but worth it. The eats are hot and plentiful, the coffee bottomless, the price reasonable, and the staff friendly.

One evening I arrived at Kay's place on Waverly Street from work, and she was excited. There was an affordable lower triplex on Casgrain Street, walking distance from where she currently resided. I wasn't particularly enthusiastic because I knew parking would be a total hemorrhoid around there and it was right across from some ugly industrial buildings with delivery trucks driving by all day long, but our terms included an agreement to see a place before turning it down because truthfully, one does not know.

She called the landlord and he said we could look at the flat, but he would not meet us there. "You can show yourselves in, the keys are in the mailbox," he said. We found that rather peculiar.

The large rental was on the ground floor. What really struck us was the odor in the air. Odor is not the right word … godawful stench is better. I had prepared for diesel fumes from the trucks. Instead the area outside the unit reeked like one hundred thousand soiled diapers were piled in the vicinity; a powerful, pungent smell of urine worse than an open sewer.

As we were digging out the keys a dishevelled older man on a bicycle stopped in the street and silently stared at us for an uncomfortable period of time. When I began to move towards him he sped away. We should have heeded that omen.

We entered the apartment to find that it contained torn curtains and damaged horizontal blinds, pieces of furniture, and exercise equipment from the former occupants. All the floors had scatterings of loose change, mostly dimes, nickels, and pennies. The kitchen was a mess and one of the bedrooms still had a number of toys in the closet that included a giant, furry white doll that looked like a *mugato.* (It's from *Star Trek* … look it up.) It was as if the last tenants left in such a panic they grabbed what they could carry and ran for their lives. The scene was akin to a second-rate sci-fi movie where the protagonists arrive at a derelict space station to find the crew gone and nothing but randomly flashing multi-coloured lights on control panels, an annoying background alarm that had not been turned off, and the obligatory line, "They must have left in a hurry … but why?"

"Andreas," Kay said, "this place gives me the creeps! Let's get the hell out of here!" as I was picking up the dimes and nickels. "Forget the change, let's go! Now!"

So I dropped the coins and we took off. Our exit from the peepee house was more like an escape; we found ourselves walking at a quicker than normal pace and were soon running as though we were being pursued, fearful that we would absorb the aroma of pure-grade piss and it would penetrate and infest our clothing, causing us to stink for days. When we got home Kay removed her footwear and ran upstairs to get her Lysol wipes, which we used to sterilize and decontaminate the soles of our shoes. Immediately upon entering her place we put our now-soiled clothing in the washer, cleaned them in extremely hot water for two cycles, and showered, stopping short of telephoning a priest to perform an exorcism.

A few days later Kay had set up appointments with places on the Plateau. I met her at one of the locations after work. The first place was just off Sherbrooke Street, in what was a surprisingly quiet residential area, but it was way too small; it would've been perfect for her alone. The next place was a bit of a walk from there, just off of Mont-Royal Avenue, near a gourmet meat shop that had products like wild boar sausages. I immediately imagined myself coming home from work and picking up some exotic meat to create one of my culinary masterpieces. That place's stock was starting to rise. We arrived a few minutes early and rang the doorbell of the second floor flat. There was no answer. The apartment's current occupant, who was looking to do a lease transfer, showed up moments later with a shopping bag. She looked like a fashion model: tall, slender, blonde, and oddly enough wearing a tracksuit. The surprise came as she ascended the stairs to meet us: We were eye to eye before she reached the top step; when on the same level I looked up at her. She apologized for being late, although we immediately said it was fine because we were early, partially out of fear she would get angry, say "fee-fi-fo-fum" and grind our bones to make her bread.

The building was fairly new, well-constructed, and smartly designed. There was a deep coat closet right next to the front door. The curved interior stairwell led to a wide, beautiful, open-concept combination living room, dining room, and kitchen with tall ceilings, which I guess she needed. Her appliances were all top-shelf and fairly new, and she was looking to unload them at a reasonable price. (The Amazon was moving in with her boyfriend whose place was fully furnished.) The front balcony was roomy and had decent privacy and the long back balcony, although shared, had a storage locker that would've been perfect for our two bicycles. There was parking in the rear, but as it turned out the owner of the building owned the adjacent meat shop as well, and he used the spaces to park his delivery trucks.

"Is he a reasonable guy?" I said to her. "Do you think I could convince him to let me park my car there if I paid him?"

"I don't know, but he is a nice guy, easy to deal with. When I want something fixed he usually does it right away. He's a decent landlord, friendly and pleasant."

While looking over the room she kept as her office, I noticed her Bachelor's Degree hanging on the wall.

"Wow. You went to William & Mary?" I said.

"Yes, I played for their basketball team."

I was not surprised.

"Do you still play?"

"Sometimes," she said.

Just then I noticed a basketball on the floor in a corner. I picked it up and lobbed it at her. Quick as a cat she snatched it out of the air and palmed it; it looked like a tennis ball in her massive paw.

The place was great but not quite there. Kay and I both felt it was a bit too small. Or maybe The Amazon's presence made the place seem too small. So we passed.

Not long afterwards we took a look at the top floor of a triplex across from Laurier Park. The owner was a thirtysomething who drove a black Cadillac Escalade. He had bought and renovated neighbouring buildings, and I'm willing to guess reno-victed long-term tenants in the process. There were parking spaces in the back and when I asked if I could lease one as well he became defensive, claiming he needed them for his construction crew.

"How long will you be fixing up these apartments that you can't rent me one?" I asked.

He fumbled for an answer, saying that City on Montreal parking stickers were affordable, and with one of those finding a space on the street would be easy.

Who did he think he was fooling? It's common knowledge that the city oversells those passes and that having one only gives the barer the right to park in certain areas, but it doesn't hold them a spot. That's like going to a restaurant and paying in advance for a meal that may or may not come. Personally, I wouldn't pay 5¢ for a parking sticker if it didn't guarantee me space, 24/7, 365. Once more we passed.

I posted on various social media platforms that we were looking for a new pad, hoping someone I knew had a line on a decent apartment. Almost immediately, a friend of mine who is a university professor in Toronto told me of an available place that fit our criteria.

We quickly made an appointment to see it. Kay said they were impressed that we were both writers.

We visited the place on Papineau Avenue on a Saturday afternoon. It was a good deal rent-wise and a block away from a huge grocery store and a pharmacy.

When we arrived we saw two men standing outside the basement apartment below, smoking a joint. Not a good sign. Kay is sensitive to smoke, especially weed. First strike.

We were greeted at the door by a cheery, thin, bare-legged and shoeless, pale young woman in a tunic who looked to be in her late twenties. She had unusually large feet for someone of her stature. It was she and her husband who were looking for renters willing to take over the lease. There were already some other people looking at the top-floor flat. She showed us around and gave us a price list of the furniture and appliances the new tenants would have to purchase from them, in whole or in part, if they wanted to live there. During the tour, I noticed some odd items, like multiple hula-hoops and juggling clubs. I asked about them.

"Oh," she said, "my husband is a magician and I'm an acrobat."

"Full-time, professional?" I asked.

"Professional," she said. "But we are academics. I have a Master's Degree in Medieval Folk Dancing, and he is a Ph.D. in Quantum Physics."

We learned that she was from Manitoba; he was an American, and they were planning to move to his hometown in New Mexico.

The place was huge and met all our needs. We would each be able to have an office. While the front balcony was small and on a busy thoroughfare (after living on Queen Mary Avenue during my college years I vowed to try as hard as I could to avoid living on a big street, strike two ... but the place was so nice inside I was starting to reconsider), it had an amazing back balcony covered with neatly trimmed green vines and vegetation, giving it a Mediterranean feel. I began to imagine summer barbecues and lovely breakfasts being served there. Closet space was ample, the main one being cavernous. The kitchen even had a blackboard. The appliances were tip top and a few were still under warranty; we would not have to buy anything new. And downstairs there was ample storage room for our bikes. Parking in the area, while not ideal, was manageable, and there was a metro station five minutes away on foot. As an added bonus the landlord lived downstairs; a good sign. Absentee professional landlords can be hard to get a hold of and even harder to get to fix something, but if they live in the building then they care about the condition and upkeep of the premises.

Kay and I discussed it and decided to make a try for the place. All of the other potential renters had left except for one guy. The five of us sat on the back balcony. It was a sunny, warm summer day and we began chatting.

"How did you two meet?" I asked.

"We met at an Ontario clown college," The Magician said.

"Oh, so you went to Ryerson?" I asked.

No one was amused.

I wanted to talk turkey with The Magician and The Acrobat, but the other guy just hung around. I was starting to get annoyed.

He had his say, what was that bum waiting for? I thought. *Why doesn't that jerk leave? Is he lonely, or trying to run interference?*

It took another twenty minutes before the goofball shoved off. Then I got down to business.

"We want the place," I said directly, "and we want all the furniture, too. I'm willing to put cash in your hand tomorrow, but you need to give us a little discount."

They were taken aback by my bluntness.

I figured they would be glad we could buy them out completely, enough so that they would chop off one or two hundred dollars from the total amount. Personally, I believe the peace of mind of knowing that all their furniture and appliances were sold and they would not have to seek out any other buyers is worth at least that amount.

After we left, Kay and I walked around the area and checked out the surroundings. Not perfect, but not bad. The best thing was that the place was going for way below market value at the time. We felt we had a winner.

The following Monday Kay texted me that they had offered us the place. We talked about it and while she did not exercise her VETO rights, she was having second thoughts about where it was located.

"Papineau is like a highway," she said, after visiting the area again by herself, "and I don't like the parks around there. It is a bit too far … I don't know … and the two guys, they were there again smoking pot. I don't know if I could live there with the smoke and the car exhaust."

I concurred with her the place had faults. In fact, I easily admitted all her points were valid.

"But we can't ignore the great price. Landlords are gouging people nowadays," I said.

Truth be known gouging is happening all the time, from smartphone contracts to cable and satellite TV fees, at the grocery store and at the pharmacy, especially since COVID came around. All the talk about the supply chain is a load of bullshit. I believe anyone in the news who says differently is usually a liar who benefits from the gouging or is in on it in some other way. I feel that rich people look for any excuse to jack up prices and the rising rents in Montreal are no different. Over 50,000 people have left Montreal since the pandemic began and there appears to be new construction all around. In my opinion, there is no credible reason for rents to be so fucking high and getting higher. To me it's all an opportunistic cash-grab.

"The amount of money you give a landlord is huge, over time. I've given the owner of where I live now over $125,000 since I moved there. Do you know what I could've bought with that? I don't want to give all my money to a greedy asshole and end up in a cheap retirement home when I'm old while they live in a luxury condo. Please, just think about it?"

"I'm sorry, sweetie, but looking it over I don't think I can live there. I tried to give it a shot," she said, still not officially employing the VETO. I knew if I was going to make my case I would have to try now, otherwise I could lose my chance.

"Look," I said, "I'm just ..."

"By the way," she said, "they're not budging on the appliances and furniture. We would have to pay the full price they're asking. And we would have to give them a cheque for half now, and the rest by e-transfer later, on a specific date."

"What?"

"Didn't you see their email? They sent it to you as well."

"Just a sec," I said, checking my email, and sure enough, they said their price and payment methods were firm. And they said it in a cold, tough, uncompromising, condescending way.

"Fuck them!" I said. "Fuck those non-negotiating millennial circus-clown whiteys! Fuck them! Fuck all of them! What kind of people don't negotiate? Who refuses cash on the barrelhead? Forget it! We're not going there! To hell with those fucking clowns! To hell with them! VETO! VEEE-TO!!!"

* * *

It took a few more months and a dozen or so places, but finally, we found our new home.

In Park Extension.

Acknowledgments

All books are a collaborative effort. For their help, advice, friendship, love and/or support, I want to humbly and sincerely thank, in no small way or particular order: Kelly Norah Drukker, Norah Maynard, Michael Carruthers, Jesse Drukker & Charlotte Henderson & Little Baby Henry, Alfred Drukker, Jeff Drukker, and the Drukker & Maynard families; Mom, my late Dad, Peter Kessaris, Anthony Kessaris, and the Kessaris & Anginas families; Michael Mirolla, Connie Guzzo McParland, Anna van Valkenburg, Crystal Fletcher, Rafael Chimicatti, Gary Clairman, and everyone at Guernica Editions, Miroland, and UTP; Mario Pompetti and everyone at Park Extension Memories; Peter Mandelos, and everyone at Librairie Paragraphe Bookstore, Groupe Archambault, and Renaud-Bray; The Ontario Arts Council, The Canada Council for the Arts, The Park Extension Historical Society, and everyone at The Writers' Union of Canada, The Quebec Writers' Federation, and AELAQ; Derrek Cauchi & everyone at Sinclair Laird School; Nikolas Klimis & Natalie Boky, and the Klimis Family, Walter Boky & the Boky family; Nicholas Bilodeau & Geneviève Roy, Maxim Roy-Bilodeau, and the Roy and Bilodeau families; the Trudeau family; Jayne DeLuca, Margo Lafrance, Mary Deros, Giuliana Fumagalli Perso, Elizabeth Flannery, Christos Sourligas, Isabelle Proulx, Lesley Carol Salter, Mark Abley, Robert Davis & the Davis family; Donna Lach, Lois Clouthier, Laura Sanders, Diane Landry, Danielle Belanger, and all librarians on the face of the Earth; Christine Trudel, Monica Holtgreve, Nancy Porter, Leola Bourget, Laura Lipic, Frances DiCarlo, Eric Bernstein, Andrew Bernstein, Magdalena Pereyra Etcheverrigaray, Chris Pomrenski, Audrée Wilhelmy, Mitch Melnick,

Michele Ciment-Woods, Erika Ciment & Michel Choquette, Saul Pincus & Alison MacAlpine, Rita Schaffer, Tommy Schnurmacher, Terry Mosher & Mary Hughson, and Jacques Filippi; Susan Schwartz, Dave Sidaway, Bill Brownstein, and everyone at *The Montreal Gazette*; Ian Thomas Shaw, and everyone at *The Ottawa Review of Books*; Richard Van Holst, Quinn Mason, Salena Wiener, and everyone at *The Montreal Review of Books*; Stuart Nulman, and everyone at *The Montreal Times*; Sonia Saikaley, and everyone at *The Miramichi Reader*; Richard "Bugs" Burnett, Sharman Yarnell Massey, Esteban Vargas, and everyone at *CurtainsUp.tv*; Elise Moser, Cora Siré, Shelley Pomerance, Lori Schubert, Julie Barlow & Jean-Benoit Nadeau, and Bram Eisenthal; Veena Gokhale, and everyone at The Tartan Turban Secret Readings; Martha Shannon, Mark Blaker, Shirley Roburn, Mindy Vockathaler, Amy Vasiliou, Isabelle MacCrimmon, Lydian Kirkwood, Zöe Alapi, Barbara Danopoulos, An-Marie Kassapian & the Kassapian family, Carol M. Davison, John Toich, Spiros Gravas, Christos Papadatos, Jerry Pimentel, and John Anastasopoulos; everyone at Barclay Elementary School, Outremont High School, The High School of Montreal, The McGill Conservatory of Music, Dawson College, and Concordia University; everyone at CBC Radio Montreal and CFCF TV; Michele & Terry Ryan, Chloe Collins, and the people of Morin Heights, Quebec; the late Richard King, Roslyn "Roz" Pincus, Hillary Mashal, Philippe Bisson, Paul Ivan Labelle, Henry Schaffer, John Asfour, France Poirier, Jake Brown, Marc Gervais, Harry Hill, Roger Khazoum, David Grey, Sheila Lanthier O'Connor, and Danielle Choquette, (your friendships will not be forgotten); all the people who bought, read, checked out, "liked" & reposted, shared, and otherwise supported *The Butcher of Park Ex*; and of course the people of Park Extension past, present and future…this one's for all of you as well.

About the Author

ANDREAS KESSARIS grew up in Montreal's Park Extension district, the son of Greek immigrants. He graduated from Dawson College and Concordia University, earning a BA in Communications & English. His column, *Read On! with Andreas Kessaris* was a popular feature in the West-End community paper *The Local Herald*. His writing has appeared on Suite101.com, in the literary journal *The Write Place*, and on the Montreal entertainment website Curtainsup.tv, *The Miramichi Reader*, and in *The Montreal Review of Books*. His first book, *The Butcher of Park Ex and Other Semi-Truthful Tales*, was released in 2020 to great acclaim. He lives in Montreal with his partner. Follow him on Bluesky (@akessaris.bsky.social) or on Instagram (andreas_kessaris).

Printed by Imprimerie Gauvin
Gatineau, Québec

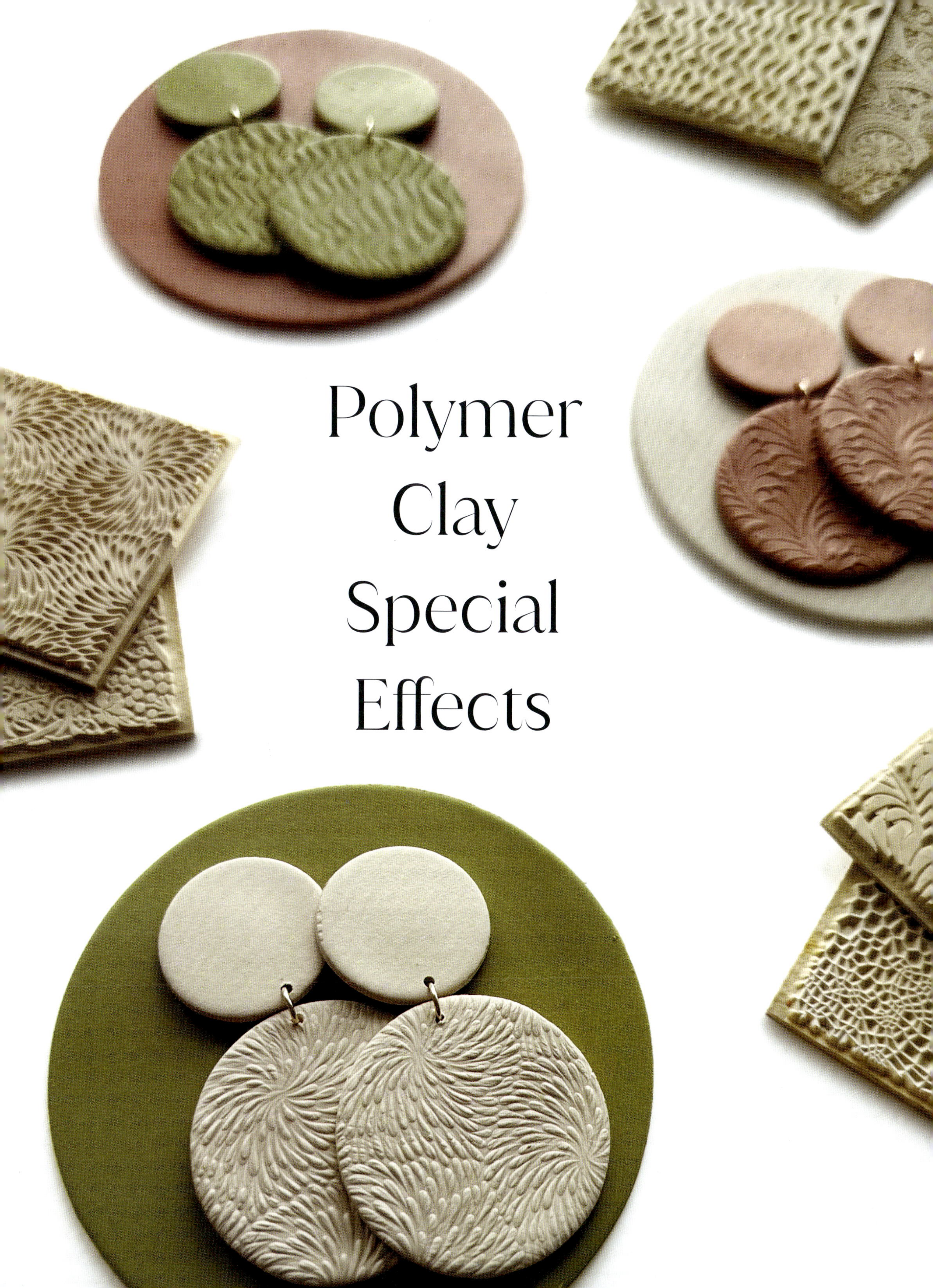
Polymer
Clay
Special
Effects